Discovering and *Developing*

TALENTS

in **Spanish-Speaking Students**

D1607358

I am not
you
I am
another tongue
land
and skin
Do you know me?
The red earth
rises to greet me
Old tales
ripened by time
sail across the oceans
to find me
like memories of
song
spice
and sweet mango trees
One day
I too shall rise strong
and proud
with the sun under my feet
my hands full of stars
and hopes
that you will see me
hear me
I am not you
but
I am here

—Sarah

Discovering and *Developing*
TALENTS
in Spanish-Speaking Students

Joan Franklin Smutny
Kathryn P. Haydon

Olivia Bolaños
Gina Estrada Danley

CORWIN
A SAGE Company

CORWIN
A SAGE Company

FOR INFORMATION:

Corwin
A SAGE Company
2455 Teller Road
Thousand Oaks, California 91320
(800) 233-9936
www.corwin.com

SAGE Publications Ltd.
1 Oliver's Yard
55 City Road
London, EC1Y 1SP
United Kingdom

SAGE Publications India Pvt. Ltd.
B 1/I 1 Mohan Cooperative Industrial Area
Mathura Road, New Delhi 110 044
India

SAGE Publications Asia-Pacific Pte. Ltd.
3 Church Street
#10–04 Samsung Hub
Singapore 049483

Acquisitions Editor: Jessica Allan
Associate Editor: Allison Scott
Editorial Assistant: Lisa Whitney
Permissions Editor: Karen Ehrmann
Project Editor: Veronica Stapleton
Copy Editor: Trey Thoelcke
Typesetter: Hurix Systems Private Ltd.
Proofreader: Dennis W. Webb
Indexer: Sheila Bodell
Cover Designer: Michael Dubowe

Printed in the United States of America

Discovering and developing talents in Spanish-speaking students / Joan Franklin Smutny … [et al.].

p. cm.

Includes bibliographical references and index.

ISBN 978-1-4129-9636-5 (pbk. : alk. paper)

1. Hispanic Americans—Education. 2. Education, Bilingual—United States. 3. English language—Study and teaching—Spanish speakers. 4. Gifted children—United States—Identification. I. Smutny, Joan F.

LC2669.D57 2012

371.829'68073—dc23

2012019487

This book is printed on acid-free paper.

FSC
www.fsc.org

MIX
Paper from
responsible sources
FSC® C014174

12 13 14 15 16 10 9 8 7 6 5 4 3 2 1

Contents

Acknowledgments

We could never have written this book without the many teachers and parents who generously shared their stories with us. To them we owe our inspiration and vision to bring the book to completion. A special thanks to Gabriela Vargas, Pilar Vega, and Karin Dingman for their invaluable contributions. Gratitude also to Sarah von Fremd, who affirmed the potential of this book and assisted in its evolution. For their guidance and encouragement at every step of the process, we also thank our expert team of skilled helpers at Corwin. They include Jessica Allan, Veronica Stapleton, Allison Scott, and Lisa Whitney.

Publisher's Acknowledgments

Corwin wishes to acknowledge the following peer reviewers for their editorial insight and guidance.

Lizbeth Alfaro
ESL Teacher
Lyle Creek Elementary
Conover, NC

Theresa Dewitt
ELL/Bilingual Teacher
Sheridan Elementary School
Sheboygan, WI

Elise Geither
Instructor
Baldwin-Wallace College
N. Ridgeville, OH

Lori Helman
Assistant Professor
Department of Curriculum and Instruction
University of Minnesota
Minneapolis, MN

Lois Rebich
RtI Facilitator
Ross Elementary School
North Hills School District
Pittsburgh, PA

Diane Senk
ELL Teacher
Pigeon River Elementary School
Sheboygan, WI

About the Authors

 **Joan Franklin Smutny** is founder and director of the Center for Gifted, a Northern Illinois University Partner. She directs programs for thousands of preschool through twelfth-grade bright, talented, and gifted children in the Chicago area annually. She also teaches creative writing in many of these programs, as well as courses on gifted education for graduate students at the university level. Smutny is editor of the *Illinois Association for Gifted Children Journal*, contributing editor of *Understanding Our Gifted*, and a regular contributor to the *Gifted Education Communicator*, *Parenting for High Potential*, and the *Gifted Education Press Quarterly*. She has authored, coauthored, and edited many articles and books on gifted education for teachers, parents, and administrators, including *Teaching Advanced Learners in the General Education Classroom* (2011), *Manifesto of the Gifted Girl* (2010), *Differentiating for the Young Child*, second edition (2010), *Igniting Creativity in Gifted Learners, K–6* (2009), *Acceleration for Gifted Learners, K–5* (2007), *Reclaiming the Lives of Gifted Girls and Women* (2007), *Designing and Developing Programs for Gifted Students* (2003), *Underserved Gifted Populations* (2003), *Gifted Education: Promising Practices* (2003), *Stand Up for Your Gifted Child* (2001), *The Young Gifted Child: Potential and Promise, an Anthology* (1998), and *Teaching Young Gifted Children in the Regular Classroom* (1997). In 1996, she won the National Association for Gifted Children (NAGC) Distinguished Service Award for outstanding contribution to the field of gifted education. In 2011, she was the recipient of NAGC's E. Paul Torrance Award for contributions in creativity.

Kathryn P. Haydon is an advocate for early second-language learning, and has taught and developed curriculum for preschool and elementary school Spanish programs. She has coached many high-school-age Hispanic students through the college essay writing process. The founder and director of Ignite Creative Learning Studio in Ojai, California, Kathryn is a nationally-known writer and speaker, as well as a teacher and mentor to gifted and creative students of all ages. A former second-grade teacher, she is a published author on teaching, creativity, parenting, and early foreign language instruction, and her work was featured in *Igniting Creativity in Gifted Learners, K–6* (Corwin, 2009). Kathryn holds a BA from Northwestern University in Spanish and Latin American Language, Literature, and Culture. She serves on the Torrance Legacy Creative Writing Awards committee for the National Association for Gifted Children.

Olivia Bolaños is the Coordinator of Curriculum and Instruction in the Santa Maria-Bonita School District, where one of her responsibilities is overseeing the Gifted and Talented Education (GATE) Program. She taught bilingual education for eleven years and was a principal for twelve years. Olivia comes from a family very similar to the students she has worked with. Her ability to create an atmosphere of *familia* within the school community and her knowledge of Hispanic culture has helped lead to the academic success of her students. Olivia has seen the GATE Spanish parent group flourish in the district in just three years by making a few changes to better meet their needs.

Gina Estrada Danley has been a teacher of gifted and talented students since 1997. She taught junior high English for eleven years and has served as district GATE resource teacher in the Santa Maria-Bonita School District for four years. Having had her own life powerfully impacted by participation in the Future Leaders camp at age 13, she has since been the assistant codirector for the Future Leaders annual summer retreat, dedicated to empowering young Latino and Chicano students to fulfill their leadership potential. A strong advocate for gifted education, Gina is active with the California Association for the Gifted (CAG). She facilitates the local regional affiliate's Best Practices Workshop and was selected as her region's recipient of the Distinguished Service Award. She has also been a presenter at CAG's annual conference and contributed to NAASP Principal Leadership Journal.

Introduction

Whether from Spain or Central or South America, Spanish-speakers* share a rich cultural heritage, replete with expertise in visual arts, architecture, language (poetry, stories, literature, myths, *dichos*), music, science, and mathematics. Before the Spaniards reached the shores of Mesoamerica, indigenous people and civilizations had flourished for centuries. The Aztec city of *Tenochtitlán* (now Mexico City) that the Spanish encountered in the fifteenth century was beautiful and vast. Influence of the Aztec culture is evident today even in the English language, whose words *chocolate*, *tomato*, and *avocado* were derived from their Nahuatl dialects. Maya societies of southern Mexico and Central America were highly accomplished in art, science, and math, with a complete written language predating the Spanish conquest of the Americas. Add to this Spain's heritage in visual art (El Greco, Velázquez, Goya, Picasso), literature (Cervantes, Lope de Vega, Rubén Darío, Federico García Lorca), and architecture (intertwining Arabic, Christian, and Judaic influences), and you have a people steeped in rich and varied culture. Today, you can read the poetry of Pablo Neruda and Octavio Paz or the writings of Gabriel García Márquez, Julia Alvarez, and Mario Vargas Llosa. You can explore the inventions of Victor Ochoa and Juan Lozano or study paintings by Diego Rivera and Frida Kahlo.

*In this book we use the terms *Hispanic, Latino,* and *Spanish-speakers* interchangeably. Our focus is on Spanish-speakers, since this is the dominant home language, after English, spoken in the United States. However, we do not wish to exclude from this definition those of Hispanic heritage who speak Portuguese or indigenous languages. According to a 2010 Census brief, *Hispanic* or *Latino* refers to a person of Cuban, Mexican, Puerto Rican, South or Central American, or other Spanish culture or origin, regardless of race.

The Challenge We Face

Despite their rich cultural heritage, it is also true that Central and South America have suffered rampant poverty in some areas. Often, people see no escape from the cycle than to leave all behind and seek a fresh start in America. Mexican-born migrant worker turned distinguished professor and author, Francisco Jiménez, verbalizes the dreams of many with his words: ". . . someday we would take a long trip north, cross *la frontera*, enter California, and leave our poverty behind" (Jiménez, 1997, p. 1). Of course, families immigrate for reasons other than economic, such as seeking political or religious freedom or to reunite with family. For centuries, Hispanics have been an integral part of American society and culture. In the past few decades, however, immigration from Spanish-speaking countries to the United States has increased in significant waves, much like the migration from Eastern Europe and Ireland in the early twentieth century.

As the number of Latino students and English language learners (ELLs) in U.S. schools has climbed rapidly, many researchers, educators, and commentators have highlighted a staggering gap in school achievement for Hispanic students. The data show that this disparity, beginning in kindergarten and continuing through the entire trajectory of a student's education, results in a disproportionate number of Hispanic high school dropouts and low college graduation rates. In fact, the high school dropout rate for Hispanics (17.6 percent in 2009) is almost three and a half times that of Caucasian students, and about twice that of African American students. (See Figure 0.1.)

For regular classroom teachers especially, this influx has presented an unprecedented challenge as they try to juggle the unique learning needs of Spanish-speaking students while continuing to meet required state and national curriculum standards. Even those in established programs for bilingual students struggle with limited time and resources to address not only the increased population but also the varying levels of proficiency and ability in English language learners. Most teachers feel that they have more on their plates than ever before. It seems impossible to serve the diverse needs that present themselves in the classroom while also meeting the demand for higher test scores and minimum proficiency for all students.

In 2010, while significant gains had been made, still only 32 percent of Hispanic 18- to 24-year-olds were enrolled in college. This compares to 38 percent of blacks, 43 percent of whites, and 62 percent of Asians. In the same year, only 54 percent of Hispanics were at four-year colleges, versus 73 percent of whites.

These statistics do not tell the whole story, however. Thousands of Hispanics thrive across the spectrum of professions and overcome the challenges of childhood immigration, assimilation into a new culture and society, and poverty. Though many of these students slip through

Figure 0.1   High School Dropout Rate by Ethnicity (2008)

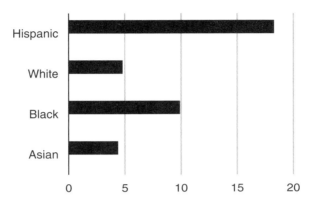

Source: U.S. Department of Education, National Center for Education Statistics. (2010). The Condition of Education 2010 (NCES 2010-028).

Note: The status dropout rate is the percentage of 16- through 24-year-olds who are not enrolled in high school and who lack a high school credential. A high school credential includes a high school diploma or equivalent credential such as a General Educational Development (GED) certificate.

College Enrollment Rates 2010 (18- to 24-year-olds)

Hispanic	Black	White	Asian
32%	38%	43%	62%

Percent of College Students Enrolled at Four-Year Colleges 2010

Hispanic	Black	White	Asian
54%	63%	73%	78%

Source: Adapted from Aud, S., Fox, M. A., and KewalRamani, A. (2010b, pp. 118–124). *Status and trends in the education of racial and ethnic groups.* Washington, D.C.: U.S. Department of Education, National Center for Education Statistics.

the cracks, some do not. Often, it is a single teacher or mentor that makes the difference. Hispanic educator Jaime Escalante of *Stand and Deliver* fame raised expectations for high school math students in the *barrio* of East Los Angeles. Jiménez acknowledged his own teachers in *The Circuit*: "I would like to express my sincere gratitude to my teachers whose faith in my ability and guidance helped me break the migrant circuit" (Jiménez, 1997). Sandra Cisneros, whose biography we examine later in the book, is another author whose teachers greatly influenced the course of her success.

The Potential for Change

As a classroom teacher or administrator of a school, you likely are wondering what you can do right now to help your Hispanic students succeed. Whether you are a bilingual or ESL specialist teacher, an English-speaking classroom teacher, a classroom teacher with partial or full fluency in Spanish, or an administrator, you face the challenge of educating a growing population of students with whom there often exists a cultural and linguistic barrier. In this book, we demonstrate:

- How to leverage bilingualism and culture to facilitate student learning;
- How to recognize strengths and talents in children even in the face of a language barrier;
- How teaching to these strengths brings tangible benefits to Hispanic students, including ELLs, and to teachers who need practical ways to assist them;
- How to adapt the tools and strategies to the unique needs of students; and
- How to connect with parents and the greater Spanish-speaking community to support this work.

Ingredients for schools and classrooms where Hispanic students thrive:

- Parents and community engaged
- High expectations
- Cultural understanding and respect
- Motivation through instruction relevant to students' lives
- Challenging, rich learning experiences
- Recognition of cognitive benefits of being bilingual
- Trusting, respectful atmosphere

Designed to be a practical resource for teachers and administrators, the book assists even non-Spanish-speakers to break through cultural barriers to build and create an educational community that truly advocates for ELL and Hispanic students. It also provides teachers, schools, and districts with practical guidance and strategies for engaging parents and the local Spanish-speaking community, thereby creating a larger network of support for Latino learners.

Our focus specifically relates to students whose home language is Spanish because these students are the great majority of ELLs in the United States, and because the achievement gap in Hispanic students' educational success demonstrates a significant need. Today, more than ever, teachers and administrators are looking for specific strategies for building relationships with Spanish-speaking communities around the country. However, the principles explored in this book apply to students from other cultural or linguistic minority groups, as well. Teachers can use this book as the basis to acquire a deeper understanding of the cultural groups represented in their classrooms. In addition, the classroom strategies we propose have proven effective with a wide spectrum of students, including underachievers and gifted learners. By supporting ELLs, therefore, teachers can also improve the educational experience for many more students.

We agree with key conclusions drawn by Gándara and Contreras (2009), that Hispanic students need teachers who:

- Can and will communicate with their parents and communities;
- Understand their unique and bountiful culture; and
- Create rich and challenging learning experiences that draw out and build on their strengths.

Both research and practical experience have pinpointed key characteristics of schools and classrooms in which Hispanic students—whether recent immigrants, ELLs, or third-generation children—have experienced educational success and growth. High expectations, challenging content, and an education more relevant to their lives enable Hispanic students to thrive. The Hispanic Dropout Project, a study commissioned by the U.S. Secretary of Education, reported a revealing conclusion:

> Students' reports to the Hispanic Dropout Project and our own observations during site visits corroborate what is reported in the research on tracking and on instructional quality of lower tracks—that is, the everyday in-school experiences of too many Hispanic students fail to engage their minds. In contrast to their criticisms of their secondary schools, many students interviewed by the Hispanic Dropout Project praised volunteers and teachers in their schools and in alternative placements who made course work relevant to their lives and, thereby, compelling enough to make them want to achieve. (Secada et al., 1998, p. 15)

We provide best practices in Chapters 7 and 8 on how to structure your classroom to provide the rich learning experiences that Hispanic students and ELLs need to excel.

Almost of equal importance is parent engagement in the education of Spanish-speaking children. Research has demonstrated time and time again that effective communication with parents improves minority children's educational experiences (Gallagher, 2007; Henderson & Berla, 1995; Van Tassel-Baska, 1989; and others). Communicating with parents and understanding students' backgrounds and motivations require a certain amount of cultural knowledge, as well as specific strategies to reach out to the greater Spanish-speaking community in your city or town. In Chapters 3 and 6, we share student stories, cultural background information, and outreach possibilities.

This book is designed to help you build on your own knowledge and strengths as an educator. You do not have to reinvent the wheel, as you most likely are using at least some of the strategies we propose. With minor adjustments, you can go further to support the needs of your Hispanic students, whether recent immigrants or not. This may require only a simple change in approach (such as adjusting choices in activities or resources) or a deeper awareness and exploration of the Spanish-speaking community. Many ideas will be familiar to you from other teaching contexts, and we translate them here so that you can apply them more effectively to your Spanish-speaking students. The strategies we propose are not only straightforward and practical, but gradual, thus freeing you to integrate them without constraining you to a system that will require substantial time to learn and implement.

We believe from our collective 100 plus years' experience in education at the classroom and administrative levels that individual teachers and districts need practical ways to extend their knowledge so that they may act right now to support these deserving students. Your own life as an educator will become less frustrating and more satisfying as you witness positive change in student learning.

1

The Changing Landscape of U.S. Schools

A Call to Action

According to the 2010 census, the United States is now home to more than 50 million Hispanics, and this number is projected to top 132.8 million by 2050. Hispanics accounted for more than half the growth of the total population from 2000 to 2010, though 63 percent of the increase resulted from births, not immigration. At this time, one in six people, and one in four children, living in America is Hispanic.

Figure 1.1   The number of U.S. residents who speak Spanish at home has increased from 11,000,000 in 1980 to 35,000,000 today.

Source: U.S. Census Bureau, 2010a.

Top 10 List: States With the Highest Hispanic Populations

	Number of People	Percentage of Total State Population
California	14,013,719	37.6
Texas	9,460,921	37.6
Florida	4,223,806	22.5
New York	3,416,922	17.6
Illinois	2,027,578	15.8
Arizona	1,895,149	29.6
New Jersey	1,555,144	17.7
Colorado	1,038,687	20.7
New Mexico	953,403	46.3
Nevada	716,501	26.5

Source: Race and Hispanic or Latino: 2010—United States—Places and (for Selected States) County Subdivisions With 50,000 or More Population by State; and for Puerto Rico 2010 Census Summary File 1 (U.S. Census Bureau, 2010c).

Demographics

In this chapter we look at the growing number of immigrants who speak primarily Spanish in the home. Considering the increase in the number of U.S. residents who speak Spanish at home from 1980 to today (see Figure 1.1), you can see why you may face a challenge as a teacher adapting resources to meet the varying needs of students in your classroom, or as an administrator who is searching for resources and strategies to satisfy the full spectrum of educational needs presented by an evolving population. The school district is a microcosm for the changing landscape of American demographics and manifests the same tensions and struggles of people wanting to assimilate and fit in without suffering the loss of cultural identity, language, and society.

Children who speak primarily Spanish at home are likely to be first- or second-generation immigrants. This demographic can be challenging to schools ill-equipped to deal with their numbers and varying levels of fluency and academic proficiency. These are also the students who may have the hardest time assimilating into school in the first place, on top of a traumatic move to a foreign country and culture. In states that have large migrant populations, such as California and Washington, even greater challenges arise when children move from place to place, often changing schools or missing classes for periods of time as their families move to find the next job.

Then there are families who do not speak English at all, parents who may not have had the opportunity for extensive education in their home countries, and others who feel little connection to schools or are too overburdened to oversee their children's education. All of this can be overwhelming, especially in the face of language barriers and student uniqueness, as well as, in many cases, poverty. These factors and others have been cited to explain a startling achievement gap even among third-generation Hispanics. Using important data points, we here highlight a number of the challenges to be overcome in the education of our country's Hispanic students. But do not despair! The remainder of this book offers information and strategies for teachers and administrators who are looking for practical steps they can take to build an effective learning environment for Hispanic students and English language learners (ELLs).

Dr. Francisco Jiménez, now a professor at Santa Clara University, describes his nomadic life as a child of Mexican migrant workers in his book *The Circuit: Stories from the Life of a Migrant Child* (1997). For years, his poverty-stricken family dreamed of California where "people there sweep money off the streets." However when they stepped into life as seasonal harvesters, cold, hard reality set in. The family lived in tents, garages, or dilapidated barracks while his father, mother, and brother did backbreaking work in the fields. Young Francisco was in and out of school depending on the family's location, his need to generate income for the family, and the time of year. He describes his shyness in class, his embarrassment to speak or read aloud on account of his accent, and the teachers that believed in him regardless of communication limitations. The book is written with an honesty that does not include bitterness or regret— simply the reality of the migrant experience from the perspective of a man who memorized English words and definitions as he picked cotton and strawberries, and, ultimately, went on to receive a PhD from Columbia University and become a professor and writer.

Figure 1.2   English Language Learners in the U.S. and California

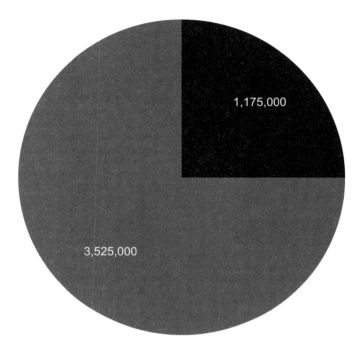

■ELLs in California   ■ELLs in U.S. other than California

1,175,000

3,525,000

> Did you know? California educates nearly one fourth of the country's ELLs. A whopping 25 percent (or 1.5 million) of California's K–12 students are English learners. Some 85 percent of these students speak Spanish as their primary language, and 85 percent are economically disadvantaged.
>
> *Source:* Payán & Nettles (2006, pp. 1–8).

Potential Obstacles to Educating Hispanic Youth

Language Barrier

The population of students whose primary home language is Spanish is rapidly growing in U.S. schools. The 35.5 million people living in the United States who self-identified as speaking only Spanish (or Spanish Creole) at home (U.S. Census Bureau, 2009) computes to 12.4 percent of our total population (see Figure 1.3). This

Figure 1.3 Chart of U.S. Residents Who Speak Only Spanish or Spanish Creole at Home

1980	1990	2000	2007	2009	Percentage change 1980-2009	Percentage of population
11,116,194	17,345,064	28,101,052	34,547,077	35,468,501	319	12.4

Source: U.S. Census Bureau, 2007; American Community Survey, 2009.

reflects an increase of 126 percent since the year 2000, and an increase of 319 percent since 1980. The numbers keep growing due to large immigration levels, primarily from Mexico, and a high fertility rate for Hispanic females giving birth to children while already living in the United States.

Many students enter school without knowing a word of English. In fact, as of 2009, there were a reported 4.7 million ELLs in schools nationwide. The majority of these students speak only Spanish at home. Of all ELLs, 61 percent are in elementary school and 20 percent are in middle school. Furthermore, of those 35.5 million U.S. residents who reportedly speak only Spanish at home, 45.7 percent of them claim that they speak English "less than very well." We can conclude by the age breakdowns that more than 50 percent of the parents of students that speak only Spanish at home have limited to no knowledge of English.

However, many students designated as ELLs were born and have undergone all of their schooling in the United States. They have parents that do speak English and, even so, have been on the ELL track for much of their schooling career. While the average time spent in an effective bilingual program is three years, it takes between three and five years for a student to obtain basic oral proficiency, but between five and seven years to attain academic proficiency. Working up to academic proficiency can account for a large percentage of a child's education, so it is important that both bilingual programs and mainstream classroom experiences be effective and supportive to the student.

Poverty

Adding to language barriers are obstacles of poverty. A compilation of data by the National Center for Education Statistics (2009b) reported that 77 percent of Hispanic public school fourth graders

> I could see how difficult it was for my mother to try and buy us new clothes for school, so in fourth grade I began to work in the fields picking fruit in the hot sun just so I could buy my own clothes and so that my mom could have enough money to provide for my siblings. This has made me a hard worker, and it opened my eyes and made me realize that I do want to succeed and I will follow my dreams. My vision is to get a higher education and to protect our country, the United States of America, the country where my family lived and struggled.
>
> —Elena, high school student

were eligible for free or reduced-price lunch, in comparison to 48 percent of eligible students in the general population. The Census Bureau's American Community Survey in 2009 revealed that the poverty rate for Hispanics was roughly 25.3 percent in this country, as compared to a poverty rate of 14.3 percent for the total population. That translates to more than 11 million Latinos living in poverty, which in 2009 for a family of four was set at $22,050 in earnings per year. The median income for Hispanic families is $40,000 per year, as opposed to $50,000 for the aggregate populace. If we expand our net of data to consider that 29 percent of Hispanics are reportedly living at one to two times the poverty level, the conclusion is that more than 50 percent of Hispanics are living in some degree of poverty.

Poverty has far-reaching implications on projected school success, as many studies have shown. It also can cause students to leave school early in order to work to support their families.

A recent report commissioned by the Jack Kent Cooke Foundation found that high-achieving first graders in poverty dropped from the ranks of high achievers during their first four years of elementary school, often not finishing high school or going on to college.

> When they enter elementary school, high-achieving, lower-income students mirror America both demographically and geographically. They exist proportionately to the overall first grade population among males and females and within urban, suburban, and rural communities, and are similar to the first grade population in terms of race and ethnicity (African-American, Hispanic, white, and Asian). (Wyner, Bridgeland, & Diiulio, 2009, pp. 4–5)

Unfortunately, high achievement is not sustained throughout even the elementary years. This results in poor performance in school that often leads to underachievement, extended placement in remedial tracks, and leaving school early.

Figure 1.4   U.S. ELLs With Spanish as Primary Language and U.S. ELLs in Poverty

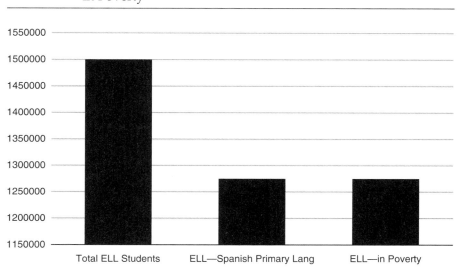

Source: U.S. Department of Education. Total Number of English Learners: 2008-09.

High-Poverty Schools

The data show that Latino students are more likely to attend high-poverty schools, defined as schools where between 76 and 100 percent of students are eligible for free or reduced-price meals. In the 2008–2009 school year, 21 percent of U.S. public school students were Hispanic, but 45 percent of students at high-poverty schools were Hispanic. High-poverty schools are most likely to be situated in cities, have more limited English proficient (LEP) students (25 percent compared to 4 percent of students at low-poverty schools), higher instances of violence and crime, teachers and principals with lower educational attainments, higher teacher-to-student ratios, and lower performance on standard assessments (National Center for Education Statistics, 2010b). Figure 1.4 shows that, while certainly not all ELL students live in poverty, a large percentage of ELLs do and many of those students speak Spanish as their primary language.

High School Dropout Rate

The high school status dropout rate (defined as the percentage of young adults aged 16 to 24 who were not enrolled in a high school program and had not received a high school diploma or obtained an equivalency certificate) for Hispanics is double the general dropout rate of all youths. It is four times that of white students and double that of African Americans. About 17.2 percent of Hispanics drop out of high school, compared to 8.3 percent of students overall. The drop-out rate is higher for foreign-born students than for students born in the United States (National Center for Education Statistics, 2010c). As Renzulli and Park (2000) reported, students are influenced to drop out by factors including race, sex, socioeconomic status, family background, and personal problems. They cited Beacham (1980) as concluding "lack of interest in school is one of the major reasons for dropping out" (p. 263).

Though the Hispanic dropout rate is high compared to other ethnicities (see Figure 1.5), the good news is that the data show it has gradually decreased over the past 30 years. But, as the Hispanic population continues to grow and if the dropout rate remains, there are major implications to our communities and economy. Lacking a high school degree limits job possibilities and increases the probability that a family will, in turn, live in poverty and at risk. In fact, a 2011 report on earnings by the U.S. Department of Education compiled Census Bureau data to show that males ages 25 to 34 who have not completed high school earn about $10,000 per year less than those

Figure 1.5   High School Dropout Rate by Ethnicity

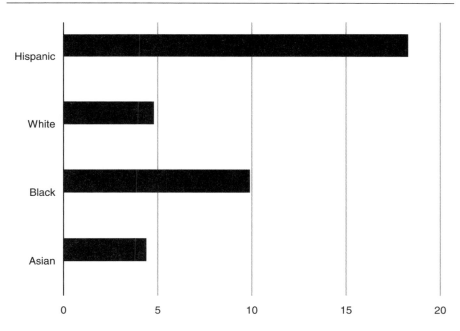

Source: U.S. Department of Education, National Center for Education Statistics. (2010b). *The Condition of Education 2010* (NCES 2010-028).

with a high school degree or equivalent, and $22,000 per year less than those with a bachelor's degree or higher. The median income of those without a high school degree is between $19,000 and $23,000 per year, which hovers around the poverty level for a family of four. High school dropouts are more likely to become involved in crime (Lochner & Moretti, 2004) or be unemployed (Caspi, Wright, Moffit, & Silva, 1998). A pool of Latino workers less skilled and less prepared will not be good for our communities or for our country (National Center for Education Statistics, 2011).

In a 2009 survey by the Pew Hispanic Center, Hispanic youths ages 16 to 25 were asked, "Why don't Hispanic students do as well as others in school?" Students responded with a combination of the following explanations:

- Parents of Hispanic students do not play an active role in their education.
- Hispanic students know less English.
- Too many teachers do not know how to work with Hispanic students.

These responses were especially strong among first-generation Hispanics, those who were born outside of the 50 states (Pew Hispanic Center, 2009). Their explanations, of course, are not scientific but do reflect the personal experience of Latino students and their perceptions of the problem, as well as their acknowledgement that there is, indeed, an achievement gap. In this book we examine ways in which we as educators can help to reverse this trend.

College Enrollment Rates

From 2009 to 2010, there was a 24 percent increase in Hispanic college enrollment numbers for 18- to 24-year-olds (Tavernise, 2011). This is good news, especially since only 7 percent of this gain can be explained by population growth (Fry, 2011). Rising educational attainment over time and the weak labor market are two additional factors that have contributed to the increase. However, the proof is in the pudding, or in this case, the graduation. The fact remains that, though almost a third of young Hispanics are currently enrolled in college (see Figure 1.6), the odds that these students will graduate are low. So, while we have seen positive growth over the past three decades, there is more work to be done.

Figure 1.6   College Enrollment by Ethnicity

	College Enrollment Rates by Ethnicity, 2010	Completed at Least a Bachelor's Degree, 2010
	18- to 24-year-olds	25- to 29-year-olds
Hispanics	32%	13%
(Native-Born Hispanics	n/a	20%)
Black	38%	19%
White	43%	39%
Asian	62%	53%

Source: Pew Hispanic Center (Fry, 2011, pp. 4–5) analysis of the October 2010 Current Population Survey.

Disproportionality: Hispanics in Special Education

Additional eye-opening data illustrate that ELLs (most of whom are Hispanic) are in some states referred to, and enrolled in, special education at higher-than-normal rates. In 2008, 13.2 percent of all students were served under the Individuals With Disabilities Education Act (IDEA) (National Center for Education Statistics, 2009a, 2010a). An example of disproportion occurs in state data from the same year, which shows that 28.36 percent of ELLs in California were categorized as learning disabled (California Department of Education, 2009b). In New Mexico, that number was 20.5 percent, and in Texas it was more proportional at 15 percent (National Clearinghouse for English Language Acquisition, 2008).

Research has shown that disproportionality (quantities of students above or below the proportionate rate) results when referrals are based on subjective criteria, such as informal teacher recommendations, versus objective criteria, such as early universal screening (U.S. Commission on Civil Rights, 2007). Numerous factors could explain the disproportionality of ELLs in special education. Teachers may feel that a student will benefit from more one-on-one time that a special education placement might afford. Some districts do not address certain student issues without a special education label, or students may have behavioral issues that cause special education referrals. Students may be falling behind on school work and, with limited classroom resources, few aides, or little to no ESL training, teachers are desperate to help the child. Or, low performance results not from a learning disability but from nonmastery of English language skills.

For Further Reading

Off Track: When Poor Readers Become "Learning Disabled" by Louise Spear-Swerling and Robert J. Sternberg (Westview Press, 1998)

"Language Difference or Learning Disability? Answers from a Linguistic Perspective" by Rod E. Case and Shanon S. Taylor, in *The Clearing House* (Vol. 78, No. 3, Jan.–Feb., 2005), pp. 127–130

Implications for Students Misplaced in Special Education

- Once students are receiving special education services, they tend to remain in special education classes.
- Students are likely to encounter a limited, less rigorous curriculum.
- Lower expectations can lead to diminished academic and postsecondary opportunities.
- Students in special education programs can have less access to academically able peers.
- Disabled students are often stigmatized socially.
- Disproportionality can contribute to significant racial separation.

Source: From *Truth in Labeling: Disproportionality in Special Education.* National Education Association report (2007).

If it is true that special education programs engender students to receive more one-on-one attention and have smaller class sizes, would this not be beneficial regardless, even if a real learning disability does not exist? The research answers with a resounding "No"! First, consider that "a 2000 survey of 500 special education teachers by the Council for Exceptional Children found that most reported devoting less than one hour a week to one-on-one time with students" (Snell, 2002, p. 2). Additionally, while some ELLs may need special services, the support they receive in special education often does not apply to their needs and may even compound the problem by placing them in classes with low expectations and less rigorous curriculum. Latino students are at risk from this standpoint, as they are two times as likely to be placed in limited special educational settings removed from the general classroom (Harvard University, 2002).

> ## Federal Definition of *Specific Learning Disability* (SLD)
>
> (i) *General.* The term *specific learning disability* means a disorder in one or more of the basic psychological processes involved in understanding or in using language, spoken or written, which disorder may manifest itself in the imperfect ability to listen, think, speak, read, write, spell, or do mathematical calculations.
>
> (ii) *Disorders included.* Such term includes such conditions as perceptual disabilities, brain injury, minimal brain dysfunction, dyslexia, and developmental aphasia.
>
> (iii) *Disorders not included.* Such term does not include a learning problem that is primarily the result of visual, hearing, or motor disabilities, of mental retardation, of emotional disturbance, or of environmental, cultural, or economic disadvantage.
>
> *Source:* U.S. Department of Education (2010).

Students are placed in special education programs under the following categories: mental retardation, hard of hearing, deaf, speech or language impairment, visual impairment, emotional disturbance, orthopedic impairment, other health impairment, deaf/blindness, multiple disability, autism, traumatic brain injury, and specific learning disability (SLD). Children labeled with SLD account for more than half of students served under IDEA (National Center for Education Statistics, 2010a).

The federal definition of SLD is detailed in the box above. Each state has its own definition as well. According to a National Research Center on Learning Disabilities (2007) white paper, SLD is overidentified due to a number of factors, including inconsistency in definition and identification processes. A 2002 report to the President's Commission for Excellence in Special Education confirmed that:

> [T]he lack of consistently applied diagnostic criteria for SLD makes it possible to diagnose almost any low- or under-achieving child as SLD depending on resources and other local considerations. . . . To the extent that teachers are not prepared to manage behavior or instruct those with learning characteristics that make them "at risk" in general education, minority children will be more likely to be referred. (p. 25)

I am the daughter of Mexican parents and the ninth of eleven children. My parents never had a formal education and did not speak English when they first came to the United States. I was an English language learner and misplaced into special education along with a number of my peers. I later was placed into the gifted and talented program. Because there were no bilingual interpreters, my parents did not attend school conferences and could never assist with homework due to the language barrier and work schedule. My parents expected that Spanish would be spoken at home and that English was to be spoken in school. When I became a principal of a school of more than 95 percent English language learners, mostly Hispanic, I knew that we as a school needed to make sure parents understood how our school system worked. Many of the teachers and I were fortunate to know Spanish and our school site council meetings turned into opportunities for us as a school to provide parent education. The number of parents attending meetings went from 10 to more than 100 parents on a monthly basis. The comfort in speaking to teachers and an administrator that spoke their language and came from a similar upbringing was reassuring to them. We became somebody they could trust. There was no hesitation in our minds that these parents were eager to learn. These parents cared about the success of their children and these parents wanted to be involved.

—Olivia Bolaños, coauthor and school administrator

This report also found that 80 percent of students labeled with SLD are thus diagnosed "simply because they haven't learned to read" (p. 3).

This trend in high-Hispanic instances of SLD is highlighted by individual state data. The data report that 51 percent of students enrolled in special education in California are Hispanic (California Department of Education, 2009b). That is close to proportionate since the population of Hispanic students comprises 49 percent of the overall school population in the state. However, a closer analysis of the disability breakdowns clarifies that Hispanic students in California are more than two and a half times as likely to be labeled with SLD than are white students, and they are one and a half times more likely to be labeled with SLD than all other races combined (i.e., the other half of the student body). SLD is an example of a learning disability categorization that is based largely on subjective measures, versus blindness or deafness, which are clearly objective. The overrepresentation of Hispanics in this category suggests that educators must take great care in assessing student ability or disability, as the case may be.

Having said all this, there is a converse issue of underrepresentation of ELL students in special education in some districts or states. Sometimes it is the "haves"—families who can hire an outside advocate for their children—that end up benefiting from services. This issue again points to the need for clearer definitions, accurate assessments, and understanding of individuals and cultural contexts.

Underrepresentation in Gifted Programs

Simultaneously, the data reveal that nationally, 6.4 percent of all students are enrolled in gifted programs while only 1.4 percent of ELL students are enrolled in these programs (Hopstock & Stephenson, 2003). In school year 2009–2010 in Oregon (which has had a 114 percent growth in its Hispanic student population since 1999), Hispanics comprised only 2 percent of the Talented and Gifted (TAG) population but 7 percent overall (Oregon Department of Education, 2010). In California, while Hispanic students represented almost half of the student body, they only made up 30.6 percent of Gifted and Talented Education (GATE) students in 2008 and 2009 (California Department of Education, 2009a). These numbers are troubling when we consider that every child's future depends on being accurately assessed and placed in a program that best fosters his growth and achievement.

Many theories explain why minorities or low socioeconomic status students are underrepresented in gifted programs (Clark, 2007).

Carol Ann Tomlinson comments on the importance of understanding student *affect*, or attitudes toward and about school and their own possibilities for achievement, as it relates to disproportionality of minority students (overrepresentation in special education, underrepresentation in gifted programs):

> Students of color and poverty hear the message clearly, "Achievement is not really yours. This won't work for you." . . . It is reiterated when school does not connect with my language, my neighborhood, my family, and so on. It is likely that understanding the imperative of building affective bridges to cognitive achievement for bright kids from low economic and minority backgrounds is our next step in the very steep learning curve for educators who truly care to make schools and classrooms doorways to self-actualization for all who come our way. (Tomlinson, 2002, p. 41)

Most likely the phenomenon stems from a combination of factors. Carolyn M. Callahan (2005), professor in the Curry School of Education at the University of Virginia, frames the issue in this way:

> [T]he more common belief is that there are few students who come from ethnic minority groups or from families in poverty who are capable of developing into gifted children and adults or of exhibiting gifted behaviors. . . . As a consequence, the focus of instruction for these children becomes mired in low-level, drill-and-kill practice of mundane, uninteresting, and unmotivating learning tasks. The children in these classrooms are never exposed to and are not given the opportunity to explore their ability to be creative, critical, analytic, and high-level thinkers and problem solvers in the school environment. (p. 99)

The recommendation to test a child for qualification in a gifted program generally comes from one of two people: a teacher or a parent. If intelligence knows no ethnic bounds, why are the rates of Hispanic enrollment in gifted programs so low?

Barriers to Entry

There are a number of possible reasons why teachers or parents may not recommend Hispanic students for testing, or why students do not qualify:

- Hispanic parents are unaware of the characteristics of gifted children, how to identify these in their children, and the program opportunities available for a child manifesting these characteristics.
- Schools have been unable to cross the language or cultural barrier to educate teachers on identifying the strengths of their bright but limited English proficient (LEP) students.
- The pattern of low achievement that has been observed from an early age among Hispanic youth precludes them from even being considered for such programs. Teachers and schools may not know that more than half of gifted students are not high achieving in school.
- Educators and administrators mistakenly equate fluency in English with high intelligence. We have encountered well-respected colleagues who feel that even if students are highly intelligent, they do not belong in any kind of gifted program until they master English.

- The district's qualification criteria are limited, and tests do not take into account linguistic or cultural bias.
- Some characteristics of gifted children may be mistaken, through lack of knowledge or genuine confusion, for signs of a learning disability. Many cases of misdiagnoses of gifted children have been documented. Traits and behaviors commonly manifested by gifted children have often been mistaken for autism, Asperger's syndrome, or attention deficit hyperactivity disorder (ADHD).

Why Hispanic Enrollment in Gifted Programs Matters

When we consider the achievement gap from the standpoint that many ELL or special education programs focus on basic, rote skills, we can see why motivation might wane for children whose learning is centered on such approaches. At the same time, basic skills are vital for academic achievement, and teachers face major challenges trying to bring to competency students who lack the English language skills they need to perform well. So, how does one strike a balance between drawing out talents, creating higher-level learning opportunities, and providing an environment for basic skill mastery?

Putting the Puzzle Together

The challenges are clear: an influx of students who do not speak English at home, unresolved language and socioeconomic barriers, an excessive high school dropout rate, and low enrollment in gifted education programs. Top these with lack of, or at least weak, professional development for teachers in these areas. The odds seem stacked against Hispanic youth from the outset, and perhaps they are if we look at the problem from the typical vantage point. But in this book we approach the issue with practical ideas that individual teachers, schools, and districts can immediately use to work toward success with their Spanish-speaking students. The first step is in understanding the benefits of being bilingual and how children acquire a second language.

Thinking Questions

1. What challenges have you encountered in your classroom or district that have stifled effective education for Spanish-speaking students?

2. What solutions have innovative teachers or administrators used to overcome these?

2

Bilingualism

A Cognitive Strength

As a hawk flieth not high with one wing, even so a man reacheth not to excellence with one tongue.

—Roger Ascham (1515–1568)

Typically educators think, "This child is at a disadvantage because she's entering our school speaking only Spanish." But have you considered the opposite? "This child has an advantage because she's already speaking Spanish; being here gives her the chance to learn a second language (English) and become bilingual at a young age." True, starting school in an English-speaking classroom without knowing the language presents challenges for students and teachers alike. But defining a child's intellect by English language proficiency reinforces the mind-set that regards linguistic ability as the main indicator of intelligence and talent. Often, this line of thinking places Spanish-speaking children in remedial or special education classes when they would benefit most from solid classroom teaching strategies. According to a U.S. Department of Education report, "misconceptions about bilingualism may lead to the disproportionate placement of Limited English Proficient students in remedial programs simply because they lack full proficiency in English. This has obvious implications for LEP students with unique aptitudes, because buried in remedial programs, they may never reach their potential and, in fact, may leave school early" (U.S. Department of Education, 1998, p. 5).

> As an ELL student myself, I always thought I was "dumb" since I did not know English. I was always put in low groups and was never given the chance to show my teacher what I did know since I was embarrassed about my English. This is one reason why I became a teacher. It is a disappointment when I hear teachers talk negatively about students who are low in language arts because they are not taking into consideration that some of these students are learning two languages and two cultures.
>
> —Carmen, fourth-grade teacher

The majority of the world's population is bilingual or multilingual (Tucker, 1999). As our society becomes more globally connected, American education will have to shift toward a system that supports bilingualism on a larger scale. It is helpful for educators to understand the benefits bilingualism offers children early in life, as well as the stages they go through to learn a second language. As we recognize this, we can encourage students to speak Spanish at home and English at school. We can educate Spanish-speaking parents on the benefits of their children receiving continuous exposure to the richness of the Spanish language.

Advantages of Bilingualism

A large body of research delineates the benefits of being bilingual. A number of school districts offer elementary foreign language instruction to English-speaking children beginning in kindergarten. Not two-way bilingual immersion programs but, say, Chinese class for 45 minutes two to three days per week. Centers are rapidly growing across the country for English-speaking children to learn Spanish, French, Chinese, Italian, and German.

For example, Chicago-based Language Stars has fifteen foreign language immersion centers in and around Chicagoland and the Washington, D.C., metropolitan area. Language Stars also provides foreign language programs for more than 100 schools, public and private alike. In total, Language Stars serves more than 6,000 students per week, starting at age 1 and on through age 10. Sixty percent of the students enrolled in Language Stars are learning Spanish. These numbers and the growth of this organization illustrate that many parents are demanding early foreign language instruction for their children, either because they know the long-term benefits of early foreign language learning, or they see the importance of learning a second or third language in our increasingly interconnected world. If parents pay to send their children to schools to receive this instruction because they wish their children to become bilingual at an early age, why do we not view Spanish-speaking young children as having an intellectual advantage rather than seeing their language skills as a deficit worthy of remedial placement?

Cognitive and Intellectual Benefits for Child Interpreters

Since the early 1960s, substantial research has shown that bilingual individuals measurably outperform monolinguals in certain cognitive domains. Valdés (2003) provides a comprehensive summary of decades

Benefits of Being Bilingual

Learning a second language at an early age:

1. Has a positive effect on intellectual growth and enriches and enhances a child's mental development.
2. Leaves students with more flexibility in thinking, greater sensitivity to language, and a better ear for listening.
3. Improves a child's understanding of his or her native language.
4. Gives a child the ability to communicate with people that she or he would otherwise not have the chance to know.
5. Opens the door to other cultures and helps a child understand and appreciate people from other countries.
6. Gives a student a head start in language requirements for college.
7. Increases job opportunities in many careers where knowing another language is a real asset.

Source: Center for Applied Linguistics. (2009). *Benefits of Being Bilingual*. Retrieved from the Naduti website: www.cal.org/earlylang/benefits/benefits of being bilingual. html. Reprinted with permission.

of research that has pinpointed positive effects of bilingualism on children. These include improved divergent thinking skills, greater facility at discovery learning, and advantages in creative thinking, among numerous others, including metalinguistic awareness that is critical in code-switching between two languages. Valdés does point out that many studies of bilingualism have focused on middle- to upper-middle class "privileged child bilinguals" whose access to academic and nonacademic language is planned by their parents. Even so, Valdés's own research documents the cognitive strengths and gifted characteristics demonstrated by immigrant children who act as interpreters for their families. Child interpreters are important to recognize for the skills they are using and building, and we explore in Chapter 5 how this relates to giftedness.

Stages of Second-Language Acquisition

I once worked with a fourth-grade ELL student. She didn't speak much in class, but I worked with her individually and in a small group. It took her a while to trust and open up, but once she did, she had so much to say. This is what she said: She felt stupid and ashamed because she couldn't speak English as well as the others. She wanted to raise her hand and speak up or ask questions—she had such great ideas—but was afraid she wouldn't make any sense. She wondered if her sealed lips could make her burst or make her sick. She shared family stories with me and said if possible she would like to be a teacher some day.

She also showed me some of her poetry. She was such a talented writer! Her poor grades did not reflect her talent and intellect. Her struggle to learn English certainly made her feel incapacitated. With support, encouragement, opportunity, love, and hard work on her part, she can certainly reach her goals.

—Juanita, fourth-grade teacher

Classroom teachers need information on early second-language learning programs in order to support Spanish-speakers in their classrooms, gauge student progress, and avoid premature worry about lack of language acquisition. If you are among the 2.9 percent of teachers with English as a second language (ESL) training, you have heard of the Natural Approach to second-language acquisition, which was developed by Krashen, Terrell, and others in the late 1970s. The Natural Approach breaks from the traditional grammar-based method of teaching language and instead calls for a student-centered environment with plenty of "comprehensible input" (understandable messages just slightly higher than their comprehension level), where students and teacher have high-interest, meaningful, content-rich interactions and participate verbally when they can. Total Physical Response (TPR) is in many ways similar to the Natural Approach in that it begins by actively engaging students in content and kinesthetic activity, rather than with grammatical structure.

When children learn a second language, there is a clear evolution of development in their skills. In the updated version of his 1982 book, Krashen (2004) reinforces the point that for most effective second-language teaching, content should be interesting, engaging, and focused on the message, rather than on grammar.

If the topic being discussed is at all interesting, and if it is comprehensible, much of the "pressure" normally associated with a language class will be "off," anxiety will be lowered, and acquisition will result. As mentioned earlier, I think a desirable goal is that the student "forget," in a sense, that the

Stages of Language Acquisition

Preproduction: silent periods, listening, perhaps repeating words but do not have their own words, basic comprehension, vocabulary = 500 receptive words

Early Production: short responses (one- or two-word phrases), small vocabulary, limited comprehension, vocabulary = 1,000 words

Speech Emergence: simple sentences, vocabulary growth, still numerous grammatical errors, improved comprehension, vocabulary = 3,000 words

Intermediate Fluency: conversational proficiency and comprehension, complex sentences, good comprehension, still writing errors, vocabulary = 6,000 words

Advanced Fluency: this stage takes from four to ten years to achieve for second-language learners!

Source: Compiled from various sources, including Krashen and Terrell's (1983) *The Natural Approach: Language Acquisition in the Classroom.* London: Prentice Hall Europe.

message is actually encoded in another language. (Krashen, 2004, p. 74)

Language Stars, the foreign language teaching organization mentioned earlier, has expanded on Krashen's Natural Approach to describe the stages of second-language acquisition more explicitly and in common terms.

Understanding this progression, classroom teachers will better know the landmarks to look for as students proceed in their journeys to develop the necessary skills in English. At the same time, Hill and Björk (2008) raise an important point about higher level thinking and language proficiency:

Language Stars Learning Ladder

Second-Language Acquisition Progression

1. Listening stage
2. Repeating simple words
3. Repeating full sentences and questions
4. Using single words spontaneously
5. Using key phrases spontaneously
6. Creating new sentences
7. Asking questions
8. Creating complex sentences
9. Expressing past and future events
10. Conversing proficiently

Authors' note: Conversing proficiently can be misleading as it does not necessarily indicate the highest level of proficiency and academic vocabulary necessary for academic learning.

Source: Retrieved from http://www.languagestars .com/learning_ladder.html. Reprinted with permission.

> Have you ever seen the levels of thinking from Bloom's tax-
> onomy aligned with the stages of second-language acquisi-
> tion? For some reason, many people think that students in
> the initial stages of acquisition can only answer low-level
> questions and that those in the advanced stages are more
> likely to answer high-level questions. However, this is not
> the case. (p. 24)

This is a key point, and the crux of our position: English language learners (ELLs) need rich and challenging learning experiences from the moment they set foot in school, not after they
have achieved English proficiency. Withholding depth and focusing on rote, skill-based learning tends to pigeonhole students on
remedial tracks, ignores their individual strengths, and decreases
motivation.

Academic Language

Alejandra is an eighth-grade student. She arrived in the United States
from Guatemala during her fifth-grade year, having had only three
years of formal schooling. Her parents work day and night, and there
is no opportunity to visit a museum or cultural institution outside of
school. Alejandra's mother and father each had four years of school
in Guatemala, and they are living below the poverty line in the
United States.

Alejandra is a quick learner, and in three years she has achieved
intermediate conversational fluency in the English language. She
still makes some grammatical errors, but for the most part she is a
fluent conversationalist. Thus, she has *basic interpersonal conversational skills* (BICS). Generally for ELLs, BICS are fairly easy to attain
(Brown, 2004; Cummins, 1979; Krashen & Brown, 2007).

All eighth graders in Alejandra's school are required to take biology. Most classmates, including Alejandra, are not familiar with specific biology terminology, such as *macronutrient, dendrite,* and *half-life.*
However, her classmates do have at least a general understanding of
the meaning of words that surround the content of a biology class,
such as *hypothesis, habitat,* and *function.* To Alejandra these words are
as foreign as the biology-specific terminology. As she reads texts and
listens to lectures, she will have to work twice as hard to perform the
following tasks:

When she was in first and second grades, Vanesa spent half of her day in a Spanish bilingual class and half of her day in the regular classroom. While she attended the bilingual class, she missed instruction in English grammar and composition, but still had to take the tests. Since her performance was poor, she was placed in remedial English. In sixth grade, Vanesa took a class called "study assistance" and was fortunate to have an observant teacher. This teacher saw her spark and knew she could progress if she had adequate support. They worked together at lunch time, and the teacher monitored her progress. A few years later, Vanesa enrolled in every advanced placement class that her high school offered. She took the lead in a myriad of activities, and she graduated with a 3.89 grade point average. Holding a professional part-time job as she attends school, Vanesa is on her way to graduating from college.

- Learn the meaning of biology terms.
- Learn the meaning of contextual terms.
- Differentiate between the two types of words.
- Apply their meanings in context.

In this case, Alejandra has low *cognitive academic language proficiency* (CALP). Attaining a high enough CALP level is often the most difficult challenge for ELLs, though it tends to be easier for students with greater exposure to academic language in their native language (Brown, 2004).

Educators increasingly have focused on the importance of teaching academic language to first-, second-, and even third-generation English learners who do not have a strong academic background in their native language. When students have high BICS but low CALP, they tend to use conversational language or slang in written responses and fall behind in class. For those students to succeed, teachers need to recognize the difference between these two levels of proficiency and to support students in developing greater academic language skills. Knowing the stages of learning a second language enables teachers to provide more appropriate support structures for the ELLs in their classrooms.

Resources for Understanding and Teaching Academic Language

Selecting Vocabulary: Academic Word List (uefap.com/vocab/select/awl.htm)
The 570 words that are necessary to know to understand academic texts.

Word Generation (serpinstitute.org)
A free, three-year series of short, high-interest lessons to be taught schoolwide.

Improving Education for English Learners: Research-Based Approaches
From the California Department of Education (Aguila, 2010), an intensive process that can be used for interventions.

Increasing Academic Language Knowledge for English Language Learner Success
An apropos article with how-tos and many additional resource links.

Source: Suggestions 1 to 3 from Patrick Hurley's (2010) "Academic Language" in *Gifted Education Communicator,* Winter 2010, pp. 21–25.

Words Into Action

Beginning with the foundational belief that bilingualism is a cognitive strength, knowing the stages of second-language acquisition and clarifying the difference between conversational skills and academic language provide a strong basis for educators who want to proceed in effectively educating Hispanic students. Now that we have covered the background information bilingualism, we can explore the unique cultural characteristics commonly shared by persons of Spanish-speaking heritage.

Thinking Questions

1. Do you view recent immigrants who speak fluent Spanish but are working to improve broken English in the same way that you view an English-speaking college student stumbling linguistically through a trip to France?

2. Have you ever taken a foreign language class? Can you remember anything from it? Do you remember any of the teaching methods that were used?

3

A Cultural Primer

Familia is the very center of Latino culture. I don't feel the media has really seen that. It is the strongest thing about us and the most universal.

—Gregory Nava, filmmaker

According to the 2010 census, people of Mexican origin comprised the largest Hispanic group, representing 63 percent of the total Hispanic population in the United States (up from 58 percent in 2000). Because the majority of Hispanics in the United States are of Mexican background, this chapter focuses primarily on the Mexican culture and its commonly held beliefs about education. You will see that many of the beliefs are similar to those across other Hispanic backgrounds. By examining the Mexican culture, we provide a starting point for educators to investigate the country-specific traditions of their students.

As educators we sometimes wonder why some parents seem disengaged from their children's education. Why will they not help their children with homework? Why do parents avoid school meetings? Why do they not come to parent conferences? Why are they not more involved in their children's school? Why do they refuse to learn English? Why do they pull their children out of school to go to Mexico? Do they care about their child's education? We hope to provide the insight needed to help teachers and administrators understand the culture and attitudes of the children and parents who attend their schools.

Priorities

In the Mexican culture, education is the pathway to success and the pursuit of the American Dream. Many families immigrate to the United States with high hopes for their children. Parents feel that if their children learn English, get a good education, and study hard, they will be successful. Most families who have made the decision to move to the United States have little educational experience themselves, but they are willing to make huge sacrifices for the future of their children.

There is no doubt that most families who come to the United States seek a better life and dream for their children to be successful, and they believe that education is the pathway to that dream. However, when all is said and done, familial and other priorities often rank higher than education.

In the Mexican culture, *familia* (family) usually ranks as the number one priority. It is the cornerstone of the culture. Overseeing the family's (and extended family's) survival needs and emotional well-being, as well as keeping close ties to relations across the border, takes precedence over all else.

> To feel the love of people whom we love is a fire that feeds our life.
>
> —Pablo Neruda

Second, religion is extremely important. Many Mexicans remain closely tied to a religious background and are indebted to paying their respects to their religious patrons.

The third priority comes with what is called the patron syndrome or *compadre* syndrome. It is collaboration with one another, usually close family members, to help everyone succeed.

Top Five Values in the Mexican—and Many Other Hispanic—Cultures

1. Family
2. Religion
3. Patron syndrome (helping family and friends succeed)
4. Loyalty to people
5. Education

The fourth priority is loyalty, by which we mean loyalty to people and not institutions. This is why many families, before making a decision that affects the whole group, will seek the advice of someone they trust from their cultural background who has successfully moved up the social or professional ladder.

We finally come to the fifth priority, which is education. Yes, although the goal is to fulfill the American Dream, education does rank number five. Of course, this is a generalization, and these beliefs certainly vary as cultural shifts occur.

Migrant Director of Ventura County Schools in California, Joe Mendoza, once presented these cultural priorities at the Principal's Summer Institute in 2005. As the third author of this book listened to him present, she was seated next to an Asian American principal who nudged her on the elbow and shared that in the Asian culture, education ranks number one.

Educators often comment that their Asian students seem to be more diligent and more studious, and they generally fare better in their classrooms than Hispanic students. For a majority of Asian families, education is a top priority. This is a major divide between the two populations. Consequently, we would expect to see differences in student attitudes, work ethics, and grades. Even families coming from various parts of Mexico may manifest regional differences that affect their priorities and attitudes toward education.

These cultural priorities tend to mislead educators as to the importance of education within the Mexican or other Hispanic cultures. Educators may feel parents do not care or do not regard education as important, and they may not understand how or why cultural priorities work the way they do. The school community needs to understand these differences and to educate and reach out sensitively to the families taking their first steps into a new school culture. This education can begin as early as kindergarten or as late as high school, depending on when these families immigrated to the United States.

> The culture and language children bring to school are often disregarded and displaced, and this situation can have dire consequences. In the words of Geneva Gay, "Decontextualizing teaching and learning from the ethnicities and cultures of students minimizes the chances that their achievement potential will ever be fully realized." A teacher's best intentions may be ineffective if students' cultural differences are neglected in curriculum and instruction . . . (Nieto & Bode, 2008, p. 182)

Respect for Educators

Due to their educational upbringing, teachers are highly respected in Mexico. Parents look to teachers to strongly discipline their children, teach them respect, and set high academic expectations. That is the job of the school. At the same time, parents are usually very hands-off with homework and may not see homework as a parental responsibility due to cultural expectations and their own limited education and mastery of English. Very rarely do parents question a teacher or administrator about expectations from the school. As teachers, we need to let families know that we welcome and encourage their assistance in their child's learning process. It is a shared responsibility.

Student Behavior

> My father made the distinction between book learning and education as a person. I remember that if someone were discourteous, or if I was discourteous to someone, he would ask me if I had not been educated: *¿Qué no tienes educación?* So I came to understand the word education not as something we learned in school, not as the gathering of information, but as a way to be and to treat other people with respect.
>
> —Moctezuma Esparza, in *It's All in the Frijoles,* Nava (2000, p. 42)

Mexican parents are particularly concerned about student behavior. They consistently ask how their child is behaving and give behavior precedence over grades. There is no question that for Mexicans, it is much more important for a child to demonstrate respect, as this is a sign of an "educated child."

Many teachers find that students of Mexican backgrounds are highly respectful and so are their parents. For them, knowledge is second to behavior. This in itself has its own implications, particularly for bright and talented students. When students are respectful and

Yolanda Nava in her book, *It's All in the Frijoles,* writes about her mother in the following manner: *"Mamá* radiated what all Latinos recognize as *educación,* good breeding." That quality of behaving in the world with good manners, dignity, and *respeto,* respect for others, ultimately begins within.

hesitant about asking questions, it is difficult to tell if they comprehend the curriculum. Is it rigorous enough? Are they being challenged? How do parents know, especially if Mexican parents rarely question—and teach their children not to question—authority figures at school? Then there is the *pobrecito* (poor child) syndrome, or misplaced sympathy, where some teachers assume that the curriculum may be too difficult for English language learners and they therefore make adjustments to simplify or water down the curriculum.

Although the backgrounds of Mexicans vary vastly, they are rich in culture and filled with life experiences that many of us have never encountered. This includes coming to a new country, learning a new language, leaving family behind, and seeking better opportunities. Informing parents about gifted and talented students is crucial so they can understand what to expect from their children and the teachers, and how to find the guidance they need.

Influence of Demographics and Schooling Levels

The demographics and schooling levels of Mexican families have a big influence on their attitudes and beliefs about education. Families who come with higher levels of education may quickly learn the language and try to *assimilate* (letting go of most ties within their culture). Others may want to learn the language and make sure to *acculturate* (keep their home culture while they embrace their new culture). No doubt many of these parents will seek educational opportunities for their children and themselves. They look to community resources to enrich the lives of their whole family. At the same time, they may be more inclined to assess the rigor of their children's school work and ask for more challenging assignments if they feel this is appropriate. Most likely, they will not hesitate to question the teacher. In addition, after being in this country for a couple of years, they may question the performance of their children's school in comparison to neighboring schools. They may even move to another neighborhood to make sure their child attends a school with a higher record for academic performance.

What about families with little or no educational experiences? Can they change their attitudes and beliefs about education? Certainly this varies from family to family, but if they have a drive to succeed in this country and recognize the benefits of a good education, they too will seek out high-quality schools for their children.

Bridging the Cultural Divide

> No significant learning occurs without a significant relationship.
>
> —Dr. James Comer

If Dr. Comer's statement is true and we want our Hispanic students to achieve, this begins with the administrators and teachers at the school site. They create the relationships, bonds, respect, and expectations between administrators and teachers, teachers and parents, administrators and parents, administrators and students, and teachers and students. If we want our students to experience significant learning, we must create relationships that are welcoming, inviting, and continuously growing from the very first time students and their families arrive at our schools. Many of these students come to us with values, traditions, and cultures that vary significantly from the mainstream American culture.

Administrator Responsibilities

As an administrator, you can begin to welcome students to your school even before the school year begins.

- **Send welcome postcards.** Distribute "welcome to our school" postcards to families about three weeks prior to the new school year. Include information about the following: first day of school, class postings, arrival and dismissal times, bus schedules, Back to School Night, dress code, and the like.
- **Use an automated phone system.** If you have an automated phone system, like ConnectEd, that can call all your parents at one time, use it to share the same information on the postcard. These systems allow educators to record and send messages in both English and Spanish; as long as students in the district are identified in the system as living in non–English speaking homes, the Spanish version of the message will be left on their voicemail.
- **Be visible to greet families.** Be visible to parents and students on your school site a week before school begins. Offer a special welcome to families coming to the office for the very first time.

Bright Idea

Post bilingual welcome signs around the entrances of your school. "Welcome to our school!" and "¡Bienvenidos a nuestra escuela!"

- **Maintain a daily presence.** Be present and open to talk with families every day during arrival and dismissal times. High visibility of the site administrator lets parents know that you are there for them and their children, and it gives you a head start in building community relationships with families you will see regularly.

  > Remember, education may rank fifth in the cultural priorities of your constituents. The goal is to move it slowly up to a higher rank.

- **Use the radio.** Call your local radio stations, those that broadcast in English and those that broadcast in Spanish, to announce the first day of school.
- **Make class lists easy to see.** Prepare class lists in a large font and post them where they will be most visible for parents on the first day of school.

  > For families new to the school, find upper-grade students with leadership skills to be "school greeters." The school greeters may escort new families and their children to classrooms. Have both monolingual and bilingual students assist you.

- **Open your doors early.** Have teachers open their classroom doors as early as 30 minutes before the bell rings. This gives parents time to get to know the teacher(s), the other students, and the parents of the other students.

Parent Involvement Opportunities

Parents want to be involved in their children's education and see them succeed. Educators and administrators need to encourage this in ways that do not make them feel intimidated by not having had much schooling or knowing English well. Organize a Parent Volunteer Club. Think about how they can assist, and provide some parameters. (Keep in mind that some school districts have strict policies for volunteers, but this should not prevent any parent from becoming involved.) Here are some thoughts on how parents can assist in valuable ways.

- Correct papers.
- Sort books in the library.
- Facilitate a memory game.
- Make or cut flash cards.
- Assist with small groups.
- Create decorations for cultural celebrations.
- Listen to children read.
- Make costumes.
- Participate in set design.
- Chaperone a field trip.
- Volunteer at extracurricular events.

Setting up routines will help facilitate a successful volunteer program. Staff members often can come up with a variety of ways parents may assist. Start small and then expand.

Parent involvement also may include educating parents about how they may assist at home. At a meeting, show parents the following:

- How to read a book with their children
- How to go through a wordless picture book

When her youngest daughter was three years old, Gabriela took her to Head Start preschool. Parents are supposed to help out in the classroom for a minimum of eight hours per week, but Gabriela felt that since she did not speak English well she could not contribute much. However, she began translating documents into Spanish for the teacher, who took her under her wing. She started translating, going to parent meetings, and attending a yearly six-week parenting program. Gabriela continued this pattern of involvement with her three children, volunteering in kindergarten and first grade. In second through fourth grades she found a way to help even with a busy work schedule—checking math homework packets for the teachers at night and returning them the next day. Later, she went to meetings to be informed about what was going on with the kids and to read all the information they sent home. Says Gabriela, "The most important thing is to be active and proactive in your child's education. Sometimes I don't understand things and how they work, but I tell my kids to look for this or look for that."

- How to use music to enhance learning English
- How to practice the use of flash cards
- How to find appropriate books for their children
- How to use the Internet at the library
- How to help their children be organized

Find a local bookstore vendor who is an avid reader and knows what types of books children like and the richness of the vocabulary they contain. Letting parents know about some of the wonderful books most students love, and having the vendor come to your school site, makes purchasing these books very accessible. Researching and giving parents a list of books (see Figure 3.1) that they also may find at their local library provides another occasion for students to help themselves in choosing books.

Figure 3.1   Grade Level Read Alouds

		Book List From www.bendelebooks.com
#	*Grade*	*Title*
1	K	*Bedtime for Bear* by Becker, Bonny
2	K	*Don't Let the Pigeon Drive the Bus!* by Willems, Mo
3	K	*How Rocket Learned to Read* by Hills, Tad
4	K	*Llama Llama Misses Mama* by Dewdney, Anna
5	K	*Monkey Truck* by Slack, Michael
6	K	*Pete the Cat: Rocking in My School Shoes* by Litwin, Eric
7	K	*Pig Kahuna* by Sattler, Jennifer
8	K	*Pirates Don't Change Diapers* by Long, Melinda
9	K	*The Terrible Plop* by Dubosarsky, Ursula
10	K	*Today I Will Fly!* by Willems, Mo
11	1	*Children Make Terrible Pets* by Brown, Peter
22	1	*The Circus Ship* by Van Dusen, Chris
13	1	*City Dog, Country Frog* by Willems, Mo
14	1	*Duck at the Door* by Urbanovic, Jackie
15	1	*Ladybug Girl at the Beach* by Davis, Jacky and Soman, David

(Continued)

Figure 3.1   (Continued)

16	1	*Little Pink Pup* by Kerby, Johanna
17	1	*My Big Dog* by Stevens, Janet
18	1	*A Pig Parade Is a Terrible Idea* by Black, Michael Ian
19	1	*Splat the Cat* by Scotton, Rob
20	1	*Tumford the Terrible* by Tillman, Nancy
21	2	*Fancy Nancy* by O'Connor, Jane
22	2	*Glass Slipper, Gold Sandal: A Worldwide Cinderella* by Fleischman, Paul
23	2	*Great Fuzz Frenzy* by Stevens, Janet
24	2	*Henry and the Buccaneer Bunnies* by Crimi, Carolyn
25	2	*If…* by Perry, Sarah
26	2	*La Mariposa* by Jiménez, Francisco
27	2	*Library Lion* by Knudsen, Michelle
28	2	*Memoirs of a Goldfish* by Scillian, Devin
29	2	*Olivia Saves the Circus* by Falconer, Ian
30	2	*Velma Gratch and the Way Cool Butterfly* by Madison, Alan
31	3	*Bad Kitty vs Uncle Murray* by Bruel, Nick
32	3	*Clementine* by Pennypacker, Sara
33	3	*Crooked Kind of Perfect* by Urban, Linda
34	3	*Esperanza Rising* by Ryan, Pam Muñoz
35	3	*The Hair of Zoe Fleefenbacher Goes to School* by Anderson, Laurie Halse
36	3	*In the Wild* by Elliott, David
37	3	*Owen & Mzee: The True Story of a Remarkable Friendship* by Hatkoff, Isabella
38	3	*Skippyjon Jones* by Schachner, Judy
39	3	*We Are Not Eaten by Yaks (Accidental Adventure #01)* by London, C. Alexander
40	3	*When Dinosaurs Came With Everything* by Broach, Elise
41	4	*Calli Be Gold* by Hurwitz, Michele Weber
42	4	*Diary of a Wimpy Kid* by Kinney, Jeff

43	4	*Goal!* by Javaherbin, Mina
44	4	*Gollywhopper Games* by Feldman, Jody
45	4	*Kind of Friends We Used to Be* by Dowell, France O'Roark
46	4	*On the Wings of Heroes* by Peck, Richard
47	4	*Sammy Keyes and the Skeleton Man* by Van Draanen, Wendelin
48	4	*A Year Down Yonder* by Peck, Richard
49	4	*Young Fredle* by Voigt, Cynthia
50	4	*Zoobreak* by Korman, Gordon
51	5	*Because of Mr. Terupt* by Buyea, Rob
52	5	*Breaking Through* by Jiménez, Francisco
53	5	*The Brilliant Fall of Gianna Z.* by Messner, Kate
54	5	*The Dinosaurs of Waterhouse Hawkins* by Kerley, Barbara
55	5	*Everything for a Dog* by Martin, Ann M.
56	5	*Finally* by Mass, Wendy
57	5	*Jack Blank and the Imagine Nation* by Myklusch, Matt
58	5	*No Passengers Beyond This Point* by Choldenko, Gennifer
59	5	*Sixty-Eight Rooms* by Malone, Marianne
60	5	*The Strange Case of Origami Yoda* by Angleberger, Tom
61	6	*14 Cows for America* by Deedy, Carmen Agra
62	6	*Almost Astronauts: 13 Women Who Dared to Dream* by Stone, Tanya Lee
63	6	*Close to Famous* by Bauer, Joan
64	6	*The Dragon's Tooth (Ashtown Burials #01)* by Wilson, N. D.
65	6	*Every Soul a Star* by Maas, Wendy
66	6	*The Fires Beneath the Sea* by Millet, Lydia
67	6	*The Lightning Thief (Percy Jackson & the Olympians #01)* by Riordan, Rick
68	6	*Mistress of the Storm: A Verity Gallant Tale* by Welsh, M. L.
69	6	*The Red Pyramid (Kane Chronicle #01)* by Riordan, Rick
70	6	*Trash* by Mulligan, Andy

Source: Compiled by Becky Bendele.

All of these provide opportunities for parents to become partners with the school, but most importantly, for their students to achieve academic success. Having parents involved in your school will assist in establishing parent leaders who will become your best advocates. Finding Spanish-speaking leaders can be quite difficult, as many prefer that another person leads. For parents who have not had many educational opportunities, this may be outside their comfort zone. Empowering and sharing leadership roles among parents will help initiate that step and encourage others to follow.

Teacher and Administrator Responsibilities

When you learn a few basic words and everyday expressions in Spanish, you score huge points with constituents. Even sharing a simple *"Buenos días"* or *"¿Cómo está usted?"* shows respect for their language. You can build a stronger relationship with parents by simply asking them for key phrases or words that you will need during the year. (See Figure 3.2.)

Figure 3.2   Starter Phrases in Spanish

Here is a list of starter phrases in Spanish.	
Hello!	*¡Hola!*
How are you?	*¿Cómo está Usted?*
I speak very little Spanish.	*Hablo muy poco español.*
What is your name?	*¿Cómo se llama?*
How many children do you have?	*¿Cuántos niños tiene?*
How old is your child?	*¿Cuántos años tiene su hijo?*
Where do you live?	*¿Cuál es su domicilio?*
What is your telephone number?	*¿Qué es su teléfono?*
It is a beautiful day.	*Que día tan bonito.*
Please read to your child every day.	*Por favor lea a su hijo a diario.*
Good morning.	*Buenos días.*
Good afternoon.	*Buenas tardes.*
Good night.	*Buenas noches.*
Please.	*Por favor.*

Thank you!	¡Gracias!
Have a nice day	¡Que pace un buen día!
Where are you from?	¿De dónde viene?
Nice to meet you.	Gusto en conocerlo.
Welcome!	¡Bienvenidos!

Parents are more than eager to help you learn their language, and allowing them to teach you creates a special bond. They understand the risk you take in learning a language, and you become more sensitive to the challenges students and parents face every day. No doubt it gives parents a leadership role that they might not otherwise experience. When the opportunity for them arises to learn English, you can be there to encourage them to take the same risk.

I recall a great friend of mine who used to be an administrator. She did not speak Spanish well, but she made every effort to do so even with grammatical errors. She was not embarrassed by her poor sentence structure and usually got the point across to the parent. She was very respectful of each child and parent. There is no doubt that parents knew she cared. She cared enough to learn the language and the culture. The ambiance she created was one of respect and high expectations. Parents trusted her and knew they could ask for her assistance when needed.

Get to Know the Culture

So how do teachers get to know the culture of their students? Of course it helps when the teacher or administrator is bilingual, especially if he or she speaks the same language as the majority of families in the school. But not all educators can speak their students' native languages. However, it is equally important to know the cultural background of students. The more information you have about your students, the easier your job will be. Here is a beginning list to start you off.

- Find books, music, magazines, or articles about the different cultures represented in the classroom.
- Have students or parents share their cultural backgrounds, customs, and traditions (see Chapter 6).
- Find out if your student is a first-generation immigrant or second-generation American.
- Have students share information about the types of foods they eat.
- Have a map handy on which students may locate the origin of their families.

- Read stories related to their culture.
- Attend local cultural festivities that include art, music, and dancing.

You have to reach the heart, before you can reach the head.

—Anonymous

According to Cummins, "Teachers who wish to extend students' possibilities for their positive identity view students as cultural resources" (Yoon, 2008, p. 508). In Bogum Yoon's case study, *Uninvited Guests: The Influence of Teachers' Roles and Pedagogies on the Positioning of English Language Learners in the Regular Classroom*, she recalls the following.

One teacher I know comes from a Hawaiian background. His culture and upbringing was very different from that of his students. What did he do? He had lunch with his students almost daily and talked with them about high academic expectations. He walked home with some of the students and got to know where they lived, who their friends were, and most importantly took the opportunity to meet their parents. In the Hispanic culture, it is impressive when the teacher or administrator visits the child's home. This teacher went to after-school programs held in a nearby apartment complex, communicated with after-school teachers, and attended band performances. He was invited by the students and their parents to attend cultural activities and family gatherings. Parents developed a strong trust for this teacher and, year after year, he was the one parents and students requested. Clearly this teacher took the time to understand the language and culture of his students. The payoff was watching his students blossom academically.

I observed one teacher who did just this. She asked the ELLs questions such as, "How do you celebrate that?" "How do people feel about this?" and "What are your traditions?" For instance, as Thanksgiving Day approached, Mrs. Young (the classroom teacher) asked her ELLs whether they celebrated it in their countries before she shared the story The Thanksgiving Visitor, by Capote (1997). (Yoon, 2008, p. 506)

The insight gained from asking these simple questions and listening to the different responses is twofold: it gives students the sense that you understand and care about where they're coming from, and it provides the knowledge you need about their life experiences, talents, and cultural values.

Cultural knowledge is a key factor when considering the academic growth of these students. Whether or not you are a native Spanish-speaker, gaining insight into culture, as well as individual strengths and interests, will help you draw on students' preferred learning styles.

Get to Know Your Families

In the local community of this book's third author, many students' parents speak little to no English and have a limited education. Approximately 83 percent of the students come from families that are considered the hard-working poor and are on free and reduced lunch. Knowing this, it is important to ask the following question: Knowing these circumstances, what do we as teachers and administrators need to do differently? Here are some possibilities to consider.

- If we know that children do not have books at home, provide some or have them go to their local library to borrow them.
- If we know that children do not read at home, provide reading time for them at school.
- If parents cannot read in English or Spanish, encourage them to tell stories to their children. By telling stories, parents are developing their children's vocabulary and their listening and oral language skills.
- If parents read only in Spanish, have them read to their children in Spanish or use wordless picture books to learn how stories progress, make predictions, and develop a love for reading.
- If children do not have school supplies at home, provide checkout boxes or backpacks with pencils, crayons, paper, and other needed materials.
- If parents cannot help with homework, provide time for it at school through a homework club.
- If parents do not understand the importance of reading, invite them to learn.
- If parents do not know about the educational system, take time to explain it to them.
- If parents cannot attend meetings during the day, plan for them in the evening.
- If students only hear Spanish at home, provide opportunities at school for them to listen and speak in English.
- If school is the only place where students engage in academic talk, provide opportunities for them to do so in class.

> Only 4 percent of an English language learner's day is spent on oral engagement. Only 2 percent of that language is spent on engaging in "academic" talk.
>
> —Vanessa Gerard

Knowing as much as we can about the students we serve prepares us to effectively provide for the academic needs of our students.

Cultural Celebrations

Think about the celebrations your students, parents, or teachers celebrate in their homelands. In our area, we have many students who come from Mexico or are the first to be born here in the United States.

Mexican Independence Day is an important celebration in Mexico that honors their independence from Spain. It is observed on September 16. The United States celebrates Constitution Day on September 17. You can combine both celebrations by making it a "celebration of our culture." With this celebration at the very beginning of the school year, students and families may begin embracing the American culture and yet continue to honor their own personal culture. The celebration may involve the following activities:

- Singing patriotic songs in English and Spanish
- Performing a school presentation
- Performing for parents, preferably in the evening
- Performing cultural dances
- Having a parent-child sing-along

Parents also want to be a special part of these events. They can participate in the following ways:

- Organizing a fund raiser
- Assisting with cultural food booths (seek donations from local restaurants, vendors)
- Preparing decorations related to their cultures
- Providing music
- Directing activity booths
- Preparing sing-along packets (a great way to incorporate literacy)

As administrators and teachers, try to identify cultural holidays tied to nationalities or ethnicities that are represented in your school and acknowledge them throughout the school year. These may include, but are not limited to: Day of the Dead, Thanksgiving, Veteran's Day, Martin Luther King Day, Chinese New Year, President's Day, Cinco de Mayo, Mother's Day, Hanukkah, and Kwanza.

Get to Know the Community

It is so important to get to know the community in which your students live, as it can give you new ideas on how best to engage families. Some may live in single-family households and others in small apartment complexes with extended family members. Still others may have up to four different families living in one home due to economic circumstances. You may wonder why anybody would want to live like that. Remember, this may be better than the homeland that many families left behind.

Knowing the community includes becoming acquainted with the local churches your students attend. They can be a significant support to the school and often are willing to help when they see how their involvement can benefit local families. Some churches have after-school care and counselors who can assist the same students you service in your schools. They also can provide helpful insight into the students themselves.

Other venues that enable you to connect with the community include local organizations that provide multicultural events. These days, more family activities are being sponsored by local radio or television stations, banks, restaurants, and small organizations. You can build a new bridge with parents and students when you attend some of the same cultural events at churches, stores, organizations, and fund-raisers.

> In our school district, we hold an annual event for our students every winter. We managed to cut costs by nearly $200 just by asking for donations in the form of food and drinks. Many of our parents pulled together, called friends, and made this happen.

Familiarizing yourself with the community in this way also can help you steer families toward valuable local resources. Provide families with the information they need to take advantage of these community resources. Do not assume that they can and will do this on their own. Because you work closely with students and families, you have a unique opportunity to help them connect more to the opportunities and services around them.

Consider some of these ideas:

- Collaborate with other teachers at your school to sponsor a one-day event for students that focuses on multiculturalism and the global community. Include students as presenters, hosts and hostesses, and speakers for the event.
- Host a community resources fair. Start with a slide show that presents all of the amazing places in the area to visit, learn

from, and participate in. Some possible community resources are listed in Figure 3.3.

Rosina M. Gallagher (2007), a licensed clinical school psychologist and evaluator of bilingual education claims, "CLD [culturally or linguistically diverse] parents want respect for their cultural differences and recognition that they contribute to their children's development" (p. 7). She further identifies CLD parents' areas of need, including "assistance to understand the American education system and how to access community resources" (pp. 7–8). Connecting parents to these resources can only open up new and exciting learning opportunities for them.

Other Community Resources to Meet Basic Needs

Find out what other resources are available to help meet the basic needs of students. Where can parents go if their children need medical attention, counseling, health insurance, food, shelter, and clothing? For learning to occur in your students, you may need to become more knowledgeable about organizations that can assist in this way. Community-based resources often can offer special services to families in great need.

Integrating Culture Into the Curriculum

Children's stories written in both English and Spanish abound in libraries and bookstores today (see Figure 3.4). Most focus on the cultural experiences of Hispanic students and use English vocabulary in familiar contexts. Students love these stories because they can relate

Figure 3.3 Sample Community Resources

The Boys and Girls Club	Local community college and outreach programs
Boy Scouts	Parks and recreation coordinators
Girl Scouts	Discovery museum coordinators
Dance studios	Art organizations
Martial arts center	Red Cross coordinators
Public libraries	University or local colleges
Museums	Cultural fairs

to them in creative ways and also share them with their parents. Seeing them come alive with these stories, teachers can then build on the students' comprehension skills and background knowledge to enhance new learning. Through these cultural books, teachers can inspire and motivate English language learners to become stronger readers in almost any subject.

Figure 3.4   List of Bilingual Multicultural Books

	Bilingual Cultural Books
#	*Title*
1	*Abuela* by Dorros, Arthur
2	*Amelia's Road* by Altman, Linda Jacobs
3	*Biblioburro: A True Story from Colombia* by Winter, Jeanette
4	*Cactus Soup* by Kimmel, Eric A.
5	*Carlos and the Squash Plant/Carlos y la planta de calabaza* by Stevens, Jan
6	*Chavela and the Magic Bubble* by Brown, Monica
7	*Dear Primo: A Letter to My Cousin* by Tonatiuh, Duncan
8	*The Dog Who Loved Tortillas/La perrita que le encantaban las tortillas* by Sáenz, Benjamin Alire
9	*Doña Flor: A Tall Tale About a Giant Woman With a Great Big Heart* by Mora, Pat
10	*El Cucuy: A Bogeyman Cuento in English and Spanish* by Hayes, Joe
11	*Fiesta Babies* by Tafolla, Carmen
12	*The First Tortilla: A Bilingual Story in English and Spanish* by Anaya, Rudolfo
13	*A Gift from Papá Diego: Un regalo de Papá Diego* by Sáenz, Benjamin Alire
14	*Gracias/Thanks* by Mora, Pat
15	*Grandma's Records* by Velasquez, Eric
16	*I Love Saturdays y domingos* by Ada, Alma Flor
17	*La Mariposa* by Jiménez, Francisco
18	*Let's Eat!* by Zamorano, Ana

(Continued)

Figure 3.4   (Continued)

19	*Listen to the Desert/Oye al desierto* by Mora, Pat
20	*Mamá and Me* by Dorros, Arthur
21	*My Abuelita* by Johnston, Tony
22	*My Diary from Here to There/Mi diario de aquí hasta allá* by Pérez, Amada Irma
23	*The Old Man and His Door* by Soto, Gary
24	*Pepita and the Bully/Pepita y la peleonera* by Lachtman, Ofelia Dumas
25	*Rubia and the Three Osos* by Elya, Susan Middleton
26	*Tomás and the Library Lady* by Mora, Pat
27	*Too Many Tamales* by Soto, Gary
28	*The Tooth Fairy Meets El Ratón Pérez* by Laínez, René Colato
29	*The Upside Down Boy/El niño de cabeza* by Herrera, Juan Felipe
30	*What Can You Do with a Rebozo?/¿Qué puedes hacer con un rebozo?* by Tafolla, Carmen

Source: Compiled by Becky Bendele.

Take the opportunity to read books like *Carlos and the Squash Plant* by Jan Romero Stevens, which teaches great lessons to children, includes a wealth of vocabulary, and concludes with a recipe you can make in class (or at home), using a variety of squash plants. Another cultural story to share with parents is *Too Many Tamales* by Gary Soto. Parents, teachers, and students can read this book aloud and share it right before Christmas when many Mexican families make tamales.

Try to draw on the special knowledge, skills, and talents of parents or community members whenever you can. If you live in an agricultural community, for example, you can use the expertise of local growers to enhance lessons in science, social studies, and mathematics. You can apply a social studies lesson on supply and demand to something familiar to your students (e.g., strawberries). Have students visit the strawberry growers nearby and find out how they grow and store their crops and where they ship them.

Talk about the supply and demand of strawberries locally. How does that change with the weather? The vocabulary and knowledge students acquire in these kinds of experiences is significant. If you have a local strawberry festival, have students write and illustrate poems about strawberries, or create songs to market them.

As you can see, this is part of getting to know the culture and community of your students and integrating it into your curriculum. Here are some questions to consider as you begin this process.

Too Many Tamales is a great book to share with parents at a family literacy night. The teacher or administrator can model the reading for the parents in the parents' native language. While reading, stop and pause at certain sections to allow students and parents to make predictions about the story and talk about the words and the lessons learned throughout the book. Have parents and children then write and talk about some of their favorite tamale stories. Invite families to share their favorite stories with a group. You can then conclude the evening eating tamales from a local shop. If possible, encourage parents to come to the meeting with their own tamales. Allow some time to talk about the history of tamales and the differences based on region and local culture.

- What nationalities or ethnicities are represented in your school?
- What stories from famous or successful people are most relevant to the culture?
- What are the expectations for your grade level in social studies and science?
- What local factories or industries are nearby?
- What community and cultural resources are available in your city?

Districtwide Responsibilities

Every district has different resources available for connecting with Spanish-speaking parents. The following is a list of ways to communicate with Spanish-speaking constituents.

- Talk to key parents and bilingual parents to help get the word out.
- Share information at meetings and determine ahead of time the dates of future meetings with an interpreter.
- Provide an interpreter who understands the school system and its programs.
- Send information home to parents, through the students' homeroom, in their primary language.

- Relay information through a handmade poster or sign in front of the school.
- Find a person who can translate information from newsletters, homework, and so on.
- Send a letter home to parents in the students' primary language.
- Make mass phone calls in the students' primary language.
- Send out a mass group e-mail in the students' primary language.

Families Leaving for Mexico. In November, December, and January, many families leave for Mexico to spend time with their immediate and extended families. During this time, the children may miss a significant amount of instructional time. Following are some ways districts can help minimize the disruption to students' education.

- Modify and extend the holiday vacation time for the district.
- Ask parents to notify the school of absences so that teachers can provide instructional materials for their children.
- Have premade grade-level materials in all academic areas ready for students who leave.
- Provide plenty of reading materials for the student to read.
- Provide extended day opportunities for students.

Parent Institute for Quality Education. Parents are eager to learn how they can help their children achieve. In Santa Maria, California, David Sanchez Elementary School partnered with the nine-week Parent Institute for Quality Education Program (www.piqe.org). The institute informs parents about the U.S. school system and what they should expect during the course of the year (e.g., grade-level expectations, report cards, grading, and preparation for college).

This book's third author witnessed presentations given by bilingual speakers who understood the culture of local families. Presenters focused on the role of parents in their children's education and provided useful questions to guide their communications with the school. The Parent Institute for Quality Education also distributed binders full of helpful materials in the parents' dominant language. The whole school embraced the program and more than 250 parents graduated from the nine-week program. Parents often came straight from work to attend the one-and-a-half hour long evening meetings.

Word spread and parents came from other school sites to see what was happening. Nobody was turned away.

Teachers and support staff helped provide enrichment to the students while parents attended their meetings. The program culminated with a cultural graduation celebration. For many, this was the first time they had ever completed such an educational experience. The district has provided that program to many other school sites for the past six years.

Understanding Parents' Motives to Learn or Not Learn English

People may ask why many parents who come from Mexico do not learn English or learn it as fast as those who come from Europe. The following circumstances apply to many families who come from Mexico.

- The distance between the United States and their homeland is very close.
- No ocean divides them from their families, unlike many families of European ancestry.
- The need to go back and forth between the United States and their home country to see family is a cultural priority.
- They seek communities where Spanish is the primary language.
- They do not have access to resources where they may learn English.
- Some may not want to lose their primary language.

There is a pattern for English-learning among almost all immigrant groups. Usually the first-generation immigrants remain speakers of their home language. Their children, the second generation, become bilingual, speaking both English and the home language, while their grandchildren, the third generation, no longer speak their home languages. This has been true for most Spanish-speakers in the United States as well.

Recently, however, a study led by linguist Lily Wong Fillmore found that the second generation is showing a tendency to lose the home language even faster than in previous eras. In research presented to Congress in May 2003, Fillmore showed that even the children of immigrants now prefer to speak English by the time they are adults. According to Professor Ruben Rumbaut, the shift toward

English is swift. By the third generation, the grandchild generation, knowledge of Spanish has become effectively extinct and proficiency in English has become universal (Fillmore, 2000).

Given the opportunity, many parents would love to learn English, and they want to make sure that their children do. They understand that proficiency in English will enable them to become successful and move up the socioeconomic ladder. They know that it will open new doors for them and provide greater access to a wealth of resources for their families. But what often happens is that they do not know where to look for instruction in English. As educators, we can help them make it happen! Here are some resources that may help parents learn English:

- Library or literacy organizations
- Local community colleges or universities
- Local churches
- Online courses
- Videos, CDs, or DVDs that teach English
- Computer programs
- Tutors

A couple of years ago, many California schools applied for Community-Based English Tutoring (CBET) grants. These grants provided the opportunity for parents to learn English two nights a week and for their children to attend individual classes as well. These classes usually took place at neighboring schools and many of them were standing room only. Clearly, parents want to learn English!

I can remember that my mother started taking English classes and then stopped. I asked her why when I got older. She told me in Spanish, "If I continued speaking only English to you, then you will not want to speak Spanish." I think she was right, but she did not have to stop taking classes. Now, I know my mother did not know the research behind being bilingual, but she certainly had great intuition. As soon as my siblings and I started learning English, we spoke only English to each other and Spanish to our mother and father.

Maintaining the Native Language

Your children will learn English more effectively if they continue to develop their first language at the same time.

—Stephen Krashen

If children know how to read and understand content area concepts in their primary language, they can transfer those skills more easily to English. We do need to be cautious about what we relay to parents. Sometimes, teachers and administrators tell parents to have their children read, write, and watch television in English so that they attain a higher level of proficiency faster and do not get confused with two languages. There always seems to be this sense of urgency. But we cannot forget the strong ties students have with their parents. If children speak English only and become less connected to the family, they have lost touch with the biggest cultural priority of their community. Again, proceed with sensitivity. Children can absorb phenomenal amounts of information at an early age. Try to support families in keeping their primary language and help cheer them on as they and their children learn English and a new culture.

> There was also a time when I did not want to speak Spanish any longer and intuitively perceived which language was highly looked upon and which one was not. I remember sharing with my second-grade teacher that I did not like speaking Spanish. She informed my mother, who scolded me for making such a comment.
>
> I believe that the messages children get from the media and other sources encourage this perception. They need to have adults affirm the value of knowing two languages. If teachers and parents neglect to do this, students may lose their primary language and become disconnected from their families at an early age. To this day, I am extremely grateful for the gift of speaking Spanish and I always encourage parents to maintain their primary language while they learn English.

Why Is It Important to Maintain the Native Language?

Children who speak a language other than English enter U.S schools with abilities and talents similar to those of native English-speaking children. In addition, these children can speak another language that, if properly nurtured, will benefit them throughout their lives. In school, children who speak other languages also learn to speak, read, and write English. But unless parents and teachers actively encourage children's growth in the native language, they are in danger of losing it and with that loss, the benefits of bilingualism. Maintaining the native language matters for the following reasons:

Personal: The children's first language is critical to their identity. Maintaining this language helps them value their culture and heritage, which contributes to a positive self-concept.

Social: When the native language falls into disuse, important links to family and other community members are lost. By encouraging native language use, parents can prepare their children to interact with the native language community, both in the United States and overseas.

Intellectual: Students need uninterrupted intellectual development. When students not yet fluent in English switch to using only English, they function at an intellectual level below their age. Interrupting intellectual development in this manner is likely to result in academic failure. However, when parents and children speak the languages they know best with one another, they are both working at their actual level of intellectual maturity.

Educational: Students who learn English and continue to develop their native language have higher academic achievement in later years than do students who learn English at the expense of their first language.

Economic: Better employment opportunities in the United States and overseas are available for individuals who are fluent in English and another language.

Adapted from National Clearinghouse (2000).

One of the biggest "ah-ha" moments of the third author came from a second-grade student. This student was extremely bright and could read at a fourth-grade level. He was literate in both English and Spanish. She asked him how he learned both languages so well. He responded, "Oh, Mrs. Bolaños, when we watch television at home either in Spanish or English, my mom turns on the captions." From then on, she shared this with many other families and continues to share it when she does presentations for parents and organizations.

Bright Idea: Tell parents to turn on the captions while they watch TV.

As increasing numbers of English language learners enter our schools, it is important to develop a relationship with them and understand their culture and language, even when we do not speak Spanish. The more we learn about our students and parents, and the more we provide them with the necessary resources they need, the easier our jobs will be. Regardless of income, education, cultural background, and language, all parents want their children to succeed. Now is the time to establish a relationship with students, parents, teachers, and administrators that will result in a shared responsibility for student academic success.

Thinking Questions

1. As you take a look at the students and families in your school or district, what are some of the different cultures or ethnicities represented?

2. Where does education rank for them?

3. As you think about the students and families that attend your school or district, what steps have you taken to help bridge the cultural divide?

4. Would your students and families say they feel welcomed to their school? If yes, why? If not, why not?

4

Recognizing Talents, Abilities, and Creativity in Your Spanish-Speaking Students

We all have distinctive talents and passions that can inspire us to achieve far more than we may imagine. Understanding this changes everything. It also offers us our best and perhaps our only promise for genuine and sustainable success in a very uncertain future.

—Sir Ken Robinson, *The Element* (2009)

Cada cabeza es un mundo. (Every mind is a world unto itself.)

—Spanish proverb

From Average Student and Daydreamer to World-Famous Author

Author Sandra Cisneros has been acclaimed as the first Mexican American female to publish a book through a mainstream publishing company. Her most famous work, *The House on Mango Street*, was printed first in 1984 by the small Arte Público Press, and Vintage

Books republished it in 1991. *Mango Street* alone has sold more than 2 million copies. Cisneros has written a number of other notable books, taught and mentored students, and started two foundations that support creative writers.

Cisneros's life story, reflected in interviews and in her own writings, provides insight into the life of a Latina girl struggling to fit in but stuck on the outskirts of two cultures. Cisneros's family frequently moved between Chicago and Mexico during her early years, causing her to feel displaced. When she discovered a place that supported her passion for reading, she finally felt a sense of belonging: "When I stepped into a library, it was the first time I found a room of my own, that was made for thinking and for the imagination . . . I felt at home" (Cisneros, 2009).

Like other migrant or immigrant children before and after her, Cisneros experienced inconsistency in her education due to her family situation. She typically attended overcrowded schools in poor neighborhoods in Chicago. "My education was rather spotty because we moved a lot and there wasn't any continuity. Sometimes I would be at one school where classes were doubled up and overcrowded and I had to catch up from the last school" (Cisneros, 2009). Though her schooling was not always ideal, she highlights the important role each teacher played in her life: "Because of that disruption, it really depended on which teacher and what school I was at as to how well I did" (Cisneros, 2009).

Cisneros was an average student and she cites her fifth-grade report card that was "full of Cs and Ds." That same year, she was told to bring her mother to school. There the teacher reprimanded her for being a daydreamer. Cisneros reflects on that experience: "Now I look back and think that was a great thing, but back then it was something to be ashamed of" (Cisneros, 2009).

Cisneros read and wrote voraciously from a young age. Finally, in high school, a supportive teacher/mentor recognized and encouraged these strengths and passions. At this point her writing began to take off. She went on to graduate from Loyola University in Chicago and then obtained a Master of Fine Arts degree from the prestigious Iowa Writers' Workshop at the University of Iowa.

As a Hispanic woman, Sandra Cisneros overcame the odds, harnessed her talents, and achieved great success in life. Even to this day she acknowledges the important role teachers played in her youth. The high school teacher who encouraged her writing was especially instrumental. She did three things that became critical steps in Cisneros's education:

1. Identify, validate, nurture, and teach her how to apply her interests and strengths (i.e., creative writing) productively.

2. Create motivation for continued academic learning.

3. Provide a personal connection to school in the form of a mentor relationship.

On one hand, Cisneros's struggles through the early years in school informed her poignant writing. On the other hand, we have to ask, how might the life of this young girl have improved had her teachers identified and encouraged her strengths prior to high school?

As a classroom teacher, you have the opportunity to discover what lights up your students and makes them tick. You are constantly on the hunt for buried treasure (i.e., talent and potential) that could change your students' lives. As studies show, it is important to identify talents as early as possible because the achievement gaps increase dramatically over time. This is especially so for Hispanics between first and fifth grades. This sleuthing is not hard to do, provided you have a framework for talent recognition: a rich curriculum replete with the arts, culture, problem solving, and experimentation, as well as a stimulating classroom environment. First, here are some tools to help you get to know your students from day one. You can prepare the soil by expanding your view of intelligence, creativity, and giftedness, and learn how to assess each child as a unique individual. Torrance's *creative positives*, Gardner's *multiple intelligences*, interest inventories, and cultural knowledge can help you identify and build on the strengths of your Spanish-speaking students.

Difficult First Grade, Highly Successful Second Grade: A Case Study

Enrique attended two years of preschool and one year of kindergarten in English. In first grade, he was age-appropriately proficient in both English and Spanish. He was a bright, animated student in his early elementary years. In first grade, he finished his work quickly and was eager to move on to the next task. More often than not, he had spare time after finishing his work and became disruptive to other students. He asked his teacher what seemed like millions of questions and severely tried her patience.

At Enrique's first parent-teacher conference, the teacher told his mother that he had to repeat first grade because he was immature.

However, his mother refused to take this advice in October. She said that she would wait until April and then consider it, if the suggestion still stood. The teacher asserted that Enrique showed signs of ADHD. She said that he was moving too much in class and asking too many questions. She tried to convince his mother to have her son tested for ADHD so that he could be medicated to calm down. Enrique's teacher was clear that, if he continued to speak Spanish at home, he would not understand enough English to keep up with the class.

Enrique's subsequent second-grade experience (he was not held back after all) clearly demonstrated that he responded well to a rich, creative, challenging learning environment that kept his active mind engaged. His teacher sought to identify his strengths and discovered that Enrique loved singing, dancing, and acting. He was cast in the role of the emperor in *The Emperor's New Clothes*, and he shone. His teacher incorporated the arts, music, drama, and more challenging content into her curriculum and Enrique had a successful year by all accounts.

Now a junior in high school, Enrique has had a number of supportive teachers throughout the years. One teacher helped him discover poetry, and to this day he often enters writing contests. He is a voracious reader, plays few video games, is on the high school football team, and is at an advanced level of Boy Scouts. He is still very artistic, and he still likes to perform and sing. However, he does not get good grades. Because he easily comprehends and retains concepts, he gets frustrated with what he calls "busy work." He says, "The teacher repeats himself 20 or 30 times in the class, and then I have to do it again in homework when I already know it. What's the point?" As a junior in high school, he struggles in history and English while winning writing contests for creative writing outside of school. Yet, if you ask him, he will engage in conversation and talk about all of his school subjects in great detail.

This is a model case study of a bright, talented young Hispanic student who loves to learn but is not doing well in our school system. In some ways, he is similar to Sandra Cisneros, with his reading and writing interests. But he has not yet found a high school teacher's support to ignite his motivation or validate his talents within an academic framework. Neither has he perceived the relevance of school to his life and future. When he was fortunate enough to have teachers that noticed and supported his abilities and zest for learning, Enrique thrived. Though he has many characteristics indicative of gifted individuals, he never was recognized officially as high-ability or highly creative. Therefore he has fallen through the cracks during his middle school and high school years.

Lessons Learned: Four Guideposts

Enrique's example may seem familiar to you as a teacher. There are thousands of Enriques out there who need teachers and mentors who can support them as they progress in school. Lack of engagement and understanding make it difficult for students like Enrique to see the value in completing high school, much less attending college. In Enrique's situation, there are four key points underscored by his experiences that relate to the education of Latino students.

1. **Parent involvement is essential.** Enrique's mother was involved in his education. She advocated for him, attended conferences, and volunteered in the classroom. She also had made strides in learning English herself so that she could communicate directly with the school regarding her children's education. Enrique has two older sisters in college who actively encourage him in his studies. One sister took him for a weekend to her campus so that he could glimpse his future in such a setting. What would have happened to this child had his mother not been involved, yielded to her cultural inclination to respect verbatim all advice from a teacher, or had not understood English enough to advocate for her son?

2. **Cultural understanding is necessary on the part of the school, teacher, and parent.** In Enrique's experience, the school and teacher did not understand the implications of asking him to speak English at home. Conversely, it was important that his mother understand the workings of the school system, so she knew that she had the final say on testing and that it was within her purview to advocate for her son.

3. **Teachers need to early identify the talents of active, quiet, nonverbal, or culturally diverse students.** Have teachers noticed and capitalized on Enrique's proclivity for creative writing? He has failed English, but why has no one drawn a connection between his creative writing contests and how he can apply his interests to essays and literary criticism? Has a teacher pointed out contests for him, or acknowledged the advantages of being a creative writer? Has anyone connected his interest in creative writing to future career possibilities—and the need for college first—to inspire the motivation that could get him through the parts of school he does not enjoy?

4. **Teachers need strategies to create a rich learning environment that nurtures and brings out hidden abilities, thereby increasing motivation, engagement, and success.** Without an open learning environment that ignites their interest and imagination, students like

Enrique are often hampered. When they have no opportunity to discover who they are during their school years, they frequently settle for a future significantly below their potential.

Though her first inclination was to respect and submit to the teacher's judgment and advice, Enrique's mother followed what she felt was right for her child. She did not allow him to be held back from second grade prematurely. She continued to speak Spanish at home and did not agree that medication would solve his difficulties. The problem was not inherent in the child, but resulted from a disconnect between the child's needs and the resources provided to him.

We can see that Enrique's difficult experience was not caused by passive parenting, lackluster parent involvement, or a language barrier on the part of the parent. Neither was this a case of an academically slow child. At the same time, we have to consider that Enrique's teacher and school may have had too few human and material resources to successfully work with a growing population of Hispanic students. In the following sections, we provide the tools and information you need to support your nontraditional, bright learners, as did Enrique's second-grade teacher.

The Einstein Experience

He was not a Spanish-speaking immigrant in American schools, but he had a difficult time succeeding in school. Einstein, for all his brilliance, did not talk until he was four years old, and he did not read until he was seven. Some of his teachers considered him slow. In his adulthood, Einstein said: "It is the supreme art of the teacher to awaken joy in creative expression and knowledge."

Perhaps in making this statement, Einstein was referring to what he had yearned for in school—someone to identify and value his now well-known intellect and divergent thinking abilities.

You probably are familiar with Einstein's experience and can relate this anecdote to students in your classroom. Have you ever heard another teacher remark about a student (perhaps like Enrique), "He hasn't a brain in his head!" only to find that in a different classroom setting the student thrives? But how do we, as teachers, identify the abilities of our Hispanic students who may have become

I had one ELL student who could barely read or write. Even so, when my other kids were working on "I like pizza" he was writing—even with misspellings and major grammatical errors—about inventing a magic bubble machine to float into space. You could always tell his brain was working so far above his literacy skills. This boy moved from my group (lowest performers) to the second-to-the-top group in two years.

—Shelli, primary intervention teacher

skeptical or turned off by school? How do we help them find renewed interest, purpose, and success? Fortunately for us and our current or future students, we have tools to identify talents that students may manifest even if they do not have the basic skills, mastery of English, or the motivation to be high-achieving in traditional academic tasks.

Broadening Concepts of Intelligence: Gardner and Torrance

By identifying nine different intelligences, Howard Gardner has helped us move beyond the IQ test as the sole measure of intellect. Our school system generally focuses on the logical-mathematical and linguistic intelligences (these are the bases for standardized tests), often to the detriment of students who excel in other modalities: spatial, bodily-kinesthetic, musical, interpersonal, intrapersonal, naturalistic, and existential. Multiple intelligence theory brings to

Gardner's List of Multiple Intelligences

1. Linguistic intelligence
2. Musical intelligence
3. Logical-mathematical intelligence
4. Spatial intelligence
5. Bodily-kinesthetic intelligence
6. Interpersonal intelligence
7. Intrapersonal intelligence
8. Naturalist intelligence
9. Existential intelligence

Source: Gardner (1983, 1999) and others.

the forefront of education the notion that individuals learn differently and that teachers need to identify their students' strengths and provide a variety of strategies to support their talents and learning styles.

Torrance's Creative Positives in Disadvantaged Youth

As early as the 1950s and 1960s, more than twenty years before
Gardner's theory came on the scene, E. Paul Torrance was hard at
work studying what he termed the "creative positives" of disadvantaged youth. At that time, researchers were just beginning to distinguish between creativity and intelligence, finding that highly creative
students were not always high achievers in school (Getzels & Jackson,
1962; Guilford, 1950). Books and articles that painted a dire picture of
how schools were failing poor and minority students abounded. Fifty
years later, similar reports document these trends. Torrance, a professor of educational psychology at the University of Georgia, was certain that successfully educating the country's minority and
impoverished children was indeed possible and should be a priority.
He invented the Torrance Tests of Creative Thinking (TTCT) as creativity assessments that have consistently proven to transcend culture
and economic status, leveling the playing field for all students taking
the test, rich or poor, Latino or Caucasian, English- or Spanish-
speaking.

Torrance cites evidence from studies confirming that socioeconomically disadvantaged students perform as well on tests of creativity as middle- and upper-class students from the dominant culture.
Since members of immigrant or minority communities must employ
creativity and problem-solving skills in order to adapt and survive,
creativity is often a primary strength in minority or children of low
socioeconomic status (SES).

divergent thinking + convergent thinking = CREATIVITY

generating many ideas + combining those ideas for the best
result = CREATIVITY

To build on the evidence, Torrance worked with disadvantaged students for five years. As a result of this work, he identified a list of creative positives, or strengths that are often evidenced by talented but economically disadvantaged children.

Creative positives are defined by Torrance as "characteristics that occur to a high degree and with high frequency among [economically disadvantaged] children" (Torrance, Goff, & Satterfield, 1998, p. 17). The creative positives are essential tools because they easily can be observed in the classroom by a teacher who knows what to look for, and they provide learning experiences that enable students to express their varying areas of intelligence. They do not require tests or assessments to discover, and identifying them in a student can truly make or break his or her educational future. As Torrance says in his book on mentoring cultural minorities:

> The creative positives appear most frequently when children are engaged in challenging and exciting learning experiences that give them a chance to use such abilities. The only kind of interventions which are likely to be successful are those that build upon the particular strengths of children—their creative positives. (Torrance et al., 1998, p. 26)

He went further to identify specific creative traits common to students in low income brackets. Essentially, Torrance has provided a road map for teachers, including a list of traits to look for, examples of how these might manifest themselves in student behavior, and guidelines on how to create opportunities so that these abilities manifest themselves. Consider these traits and how you might spot them in your students. Examples of each are given based on the authors' experience.

Motivation Is Key to Teaching ELLs

Torrance cautioned that, "For unrecognized potential to become

Torrance's Creative Positives

1. **Ability to express feelings and emotions.** Maria, at the age of 7, can recite poetry from memory before an audience, with intense feeling and emotion.
2. **Ability to improvise with commonplace materials.** Luis uses any object he can get his hands on around the house to invent new musical instruments and games.
3. **Articulateness in role playing and storytelling.** José sits with picture books and imitates his mother reading the story aloud. He captivates other kids with his words and seems to embody the characters or people he is talking about.
4. **Enjoyment of and ability in visual arts, such as drawing,**

(Continued)

(Continued)

painting, and sculpture. Hannah is always observing and translating her observations into creative works of art, whether she uses paints or doodles in her notebook. She enjoys projects, and her dioramas often include intricate clay figurines.

5. **Enjoyment of and ability in creative movement, dance, and dramatics.** Cristián participates in the local Ballet Folklórico. Sarah seems to have come alive with her newfound interest in Spoken Word Poetry. Evan is always moving and seems to learn better in a state of motion.

6. **Enjoyment of and ability in music and rhythm.** Marcos sings with his father's mariachi group. Sam is highly sensitive to a loud classroom, but becomes completely absorbed in any music he hears.

7. **Use of expressive speech.** Beatrice is flamboyant and dramatic when telling stories to her friends.

8. **Fluency and flexibility in nonverbal media.** Saul is often doodling on his papers, and when you inspect them, you can see that he has created visual representations of the concepts being taught. He has a mind for taking things apart and reassembling them, and he has built a computer at home with scraps and parts.

9. **Enjoyment of and skills in group activities and problem solving.** Matthew prefers working in groups over doing assignments alone. He comes alive in a small group, seems to learn more effectively, and is supportive in helping his teammates.

(Continued)

awakened, there must be a feeling of purpose—a feeling of destiny" (Torrance, 1969, p. 72). Here we gain added insight into the relatively low achievement of Hispanic students in the twenty-first century. Students need a feeling of purpose, and they need educators to make the case for the importance of school and learning, and how education will positively influence their lives. The Hispanic Dropout Project, a study commissioned by the U.S. Secretary of Education in 1995 to examine the disproportionate number of Hispanics dropping out of school, found that "Hispanic students are most likely to learn when curricular content is challenging and meaningful" (Secada, et al., 1998, p. 14). In less effective schools "students complained of dull, dumbed down, and irrelevant curricula" (p. 26). If, as Torrance observed, minority or disadvantaged students often possess a high degree of creativity and if U.S. schools teach primarily to the logical and linguistic domains, these students' abilities will continue to be underestimated by the standardized testing system that dominates U.S. classrooms. When their gifts and talents remain largely invisible to teachers and evaluators, and they find themselves in remedial classrooms to "get up to par" on skills, students begin to question if they ever had learning strengths in the first place. They realize that what they do have is not important in an educational context, and so they gradually lose interest and faith in school. This might come in the form of tuning out in class, neglecting homework, or dropping out. Teachers need to harness students' strengths, rather than define their educational paths based on deficits such as lack of English verbal or written skills.

Enrique and the Creative Positives

If Enrique's first-grade teacher had known about the creative positives and how to draw these out, the teacher, Enrique, and his family would likely have moved him onto a more progressive trajectory. Let's take a look at Enrique's creative abilities as they were accurately observed and nurtured during his second-grade year.

Because his teacher's classroom was replete with opportunities for students to participate in a variety of critical and creative thinking activities, she quickly identified his strengths. They included numbers 3, 5, 6, 7, 11, and 12 on Torrance's list of creative positives.

- Articulateness in role playing and storytelling;
- Enjoyment of and ability in creative movement, dance, and dramatics;
- Enjoyment of and ability in music and rhythm;
- Use of expressive speech;
- Responsiveness to the kinesthetic;
- Expressiveness of gestures and body language.

(Continued)

10. **Responsiveness to the concrete.** Cristina is constantly asking her teacher to use math manipulatives because they help her solve the problems most efficiently. Her most brilliant ideas seem to come after she has been twirling her hair or fiddling with objects inside her desk.

11. **Responsiveness to the kinesthetic.** When David plays soccer, he is a graceful dancer moving across the field with exceptional skill and precision. He involves his whole body in dramatics and reader's theater. Every movement he makes seems to be skilled.

12. **Expressiveness of gestures and body languages, and ability to interpret body language.** Nancy can always sense when her teacher is having a rough day just by observing her body language and mannerisms.

13. **Humor and sense of humor.** Ruben frequently tells jokes to the class and the students always respond with genuine laughter. Samantha appears shy and reserved, but when I see the doodles on her paper I just have to laugh out loud! Some day that one will crack a joke that has us rolling. I often see a smirk on Karen's face when I make a subtle pun in class—she is the only one that gets my humor.

14. **Richness of imagery in informal language.** Susie's writing is full of imagery, especially in the poetry journals she keeps.

15. **Originality of ideas in problem solving.** Peter stands out as a leader when engaged in group tasks and others trust him and his ideas. Even though he often comes

(Continued)

(Continued)

up with solutions to what other students may think cannot be solved, they know from experience that Peter's unconventional thinking is often right on target.

16. **Problem centeredness or persistence in problem solving.** Enrique will not stop until his task at hand is accomplished. He loves the Rubik's Cube and Sudoku puzzles, and continuously tries to solve them. He often helps his classmates with their conundrums as well.

17. **Emotional responsiveness.** Gabriel, at the young age of 5, would cry at the lyrics of certain songs. He seems hypersensitive to others' feelings and emotions but always wants to help.

Adapted from Torrance (1998, p. 97).

Enrique's second-grade teacher capitalized on the creative positives demonstrated by him and his classmates in many ways.

A number of the creative positives manifest themselves in action, movement, and richness of language. Some are easy to spot in a child with limited English, but the language-based characteristics are not. This is where interest inventories and parent surveys come in, because they can provide insight into more reserved or less verbal students.

Tools of the Trade

Heat up the level of challenge in the classroom and see who bubbles up.

—Bertie Kingore, educator

Enrique's second-grade teacher leveraged the creative positives in her students as she used the following teaching strategies:

- Integrate music into classroom:
  - ○ Make up jingles about math, science, language arts.
  - ○ Use math CDs and language songs.
  - ○ Stage a class musical.
- Expose students to poetry through reading and memorization.
- Use many pictures and visuals.
- Actively incorporate hand gestures, pantomime, and humor.
- Create small reading groups.
- Develop a center system that includes listening centers and buddy reading centers.
- Share a read-aloud story with art projects.
- Read lots of books, especially picture books, to provide visuals.
- Employ a hands-on math series.
- Provide critical thinking opportunities for math.
- Build vocabulary in creative contexts.
- Explore idioms and help students create their own.
- Provide a myriad of hands-on, kinesthetic learning opportunities.

I had always been able to assess my students in their native language (Spanish) and knew their learning ability and skill level. This time I got a new student from Yemen who spoke Arabic and I was lost on how to find out how much she knew in her native language. I felt frustrated with myself. With time I realized that this student learned concepts quickly. She was not considered on level since all of our assessments are done in English and she knew very little English. Working one-on-one with her I learned how talented this student was. She continues to be a great student, but has not been tested for GATE or considered on level since she is still learning English.

—Carmen, fourth-grade teacher

Observation is the most practical and accessible way to assess student strengths. In the right environment, these abilities will manifest themselves daily. What additional tools at a classroom teacher's disposal can aid in this process?

Interest Inventories

Perhaps the simplest and easiest step you can take to get to know your students on a deeper level, aside from sitting down with each of them, is to give them a simple interest inventory. (See Chapter 6 for further discussion on interest inventories). You can administer interest inventories verbally to your class at the beginning of the year, or you can have students work on them independently. It takes no more than 15 minutes. Junior high teachers who have upward of 150 students can still use this strategy and not feel overwhelmed. Take the time to administer them, glance through the responses class by class, jot down common interests that surface, and mark these in your plan book. File the student responses away and, when you have a student with whom you feel your class or content is not connecting, you will have a valuable resource of information from which to draw. If a student has zero to little English proficiency, he or she can complete as much as possible visually. If you do not speak Spanish yourself, perhaps a bilingual colleague, translator, or even another student can help.

The purpose of an interest inventory is for you, the teacher, to gain insight into your students' interests. If an overwhelming majority of your students indicates interest in animals or space, you can incorporate these high-interest topics into your core curriculum throughout the year. If there is a concept that you have difficulty getting across to students, check their interest inventories and incorporate a high-interest example. For instance, if you are making little progress teaching the concept of multiplication to one of your students, but you know she loves nature, you can use various groupings of leaves from outside to demonstrate sets of numbers. If you have a child who loves music but cannot understand skip counting, you can employ movement and songs to help him master this. Perhaps your world history student loves art but does not seem to comprehend a timeline of events; you can use period paintings and drawings to connect the student to the content with further depth and relevance. After administering interest inventories, reviewing them, and indicating students' interests in your planner, use these inventories as the foundation stones for student portfolios.

Portfolios

Bertie Kingore has been a consistent expert voice promoting the value of student portfolios to illustrate and assess abilities and giftedness. Portfolios represent a collection of student work that catalogs individual student development over time. Many districts evaluate portfolios as part of their gifted identification process. Here, we maintain that setting up a portfolio in your classroom for each individual student will help provide insight into the strengths, weaknesses, and progress of all of them over time. Students can manage their own portfolios to save you time if you set up a file folder with each student's name in a standing rack or file cabinet in your classroom. As you hand back papers, you can include a special marking or sticker indicating to the student to save the work in his or her portfolio. Middle school teachers can include research papers, responses to creative writing prompts, and photographs of well-done projects. You may not be able to keep a portfolio for all of your junior high students, but you can at least set them up for low-performing students or those in whom you see a creative spark for certain types of assignments but not across the board. A portfolio is especially valuable for those students whose talents or abilities become masked in the typical classroom, or behind the barrier of language proficiency. Callahan (2005) suggests including in portfolios examples of how students respond to high-level curriculum. When they are kept up-to-date, portfolios can aid you in evaluations, provide visuals for parent-teacher conferences, and document

---

Examples of Items to Include in Student Portfolios

- Student interest inventory
- Work that demonstrates depth and complexity
- Examples of student responses to high-level curriculum
- Evidence of ability outside the classroom (e.g., accordion player in mariachi band, translator for family, star soccer play, family cook, animal caretaker)
- Examples of written work (one piece from beginning of year and additional to show progress, or especially detailed, creative, or excellent work)
- Art work (a self-portrait created every year will show artistic growth)
- Self-reflections on student work
- Photos of exceptional or notable school projects or posters
- Lists of books read
- Recordings of musical talent

---

evidence of growth and achievement when you recommend a child for gifted programming.

Parental Input

Sometimes you need to go further than classroom observation. Creative students often behave differently at school than they do at home, and parents can provide valuable insight. Chapter 6 provides you with best practices on how to manage the information obtained from families. It also discusses how to overcome potential roadblocks if your students' parents do not speak English.

On the other hand, parents in culturally diverse populations may not have the resources or knowledge to connect talents they see at home to academics and school. Sometimes, creative achievements go unacknowledged, which makes it more important for teachers to recognize and point them out to students. Otherwise, children may draw opposite, detrimental conclusions about themselves and their potential for success or failure in school.

We must reject the assumption that deficiencies motivate proper behavior and instead accept the more realistic belief that giving attention to successful behavior motivates the attainment of potential. This means recognizing, acknowledging, and using their potential to build success, skills, and

abilities rather than wasting energy and resources by focusing
on their deficits and neglecting their strengths

—E. Paul Torrance (Torrance et al., 1998, p. vi)

Torrance Tests of Creative Thinking

As noted earlier, E. Paul Torrance spent years working with low
socioeconomic status students and developing the Torrance Tests of
Creative Thinking to overcome assessments that require dominant
culture exposure or language. The Figural TTCT: *Thinking Creatively
With Pictures* is a tool that all teachers can use. They can administer it,
without specific training, to students from kindergarten through
adults, in 30 minutes, one-on-one, or in a whole-group setting.
Relatively inexpensive to purchase and available in both English and
Spanish, it is strictly a nonverbal, pictorial measure of creative thinking skills. The scoring report provides a comprehensive assessment of
thirteen creative thinking skills, five overall mental functions, and
comparisons to national and local norms. The TTCT is especially
helpful if you suspect you have a highly creative student who is nonverbal or is limited English proficient.

Teachers can blanket test all students, or only test specific students who are not performing or in whom they recognize higher
potential than is expressed on classwork. The Spanish version of the
TTCT figural test is ideal for Spanish-speakers at any grade level, and
it can provide insight into the thinking capabilities of the students
who arrive at your classroom door not speaking a word of English.

Next Steps

First and foremost, we hope this chapter helped reinforce your understanding of the myriad ways in which intelligence is manifested by
students, especially minority students, in classroom settings. You are
now equipped to find the Torrance creative positives in your students
by means of observation, and you have tools such as interest inventories, portfolios, and the Torrance Tests of Creative Thinking that provide breadth and depth of insight to help you mine the talents and
abilities of your culturally and linguistically diverse learners. In the

next chapter, we dive into the field of gifted education so that you are prepared to find the gifted ELLs in your midst, and help them receive the educational strategies they need to live up to and develop their high potential.

Thinking Questions

1. Have you ever employed any of the teaching strategies used by Enrique's second-grade teacher to engage your ELL students?

2. Which strategies could you theoretically implement tomorrow without much planning?

The ocean—
Killer whales hunting seals
Giant waves crashing on the shore
An eel jumps out of a cave
for a fish
Whales hunting for tiny krill
Jelly fish floating up to the air
Baby turtles hatching, running
to the ocean
Chased by seagulls trying to eat them
Welcome, welcome . . . to the sea.

—Miguel, Grade 2

5

Identifying Gifted Hispanic Students

Creativeness should always be one of the criteria in searching for giftedness in the economically disadvantaged, because: creativity is a key characteristic of almost every person who has made outstanding social contributions, and creativity is one of the greatest and most common strengths of groups from the culture of poverty in the U.S.

—E. Paul Torrance (Torrance et al., 1998)

Thus far, we have discussed looking generally for creative strengths and abilities in Spanish-speaking students as they are manifested in the day-to-day classroom environment. This is essential and will increase the rigor, motivation, and chance of success for all of your Hispanic students. But what about going a step further and looking for those gifted Hispanic students who are right now not identified for gifted programs at a proportionate rate?

First, let's take a look at the facts. How are America's schools serving (or not serving, as the case may be) bright students from lower-income or minority families?

When they enter school, gifted children are equally represented across all demographic and geographic groups. But as they advance in school, lower-income gifted students drop further and further behind.

Our schools are not providing low-income students with the tools they need to fulfill their potential. Nearly half (44 percent) of the lower-income students who were classified as high-ability students when they entered first grade are no longer classified as such by the time they reach fifth grade.

Our nation is wasting some of its most valuable resources. High-achieving, lower-income students drop out of school twice as often as high-achieving students from higher income families.

Source: National Association for Gifted Children (2011a).

> Educators must raise their expectations for lower-income students and implement effective strategies for maintaining and increasing advanced learning within this population.
>
> *Source:* Wyner, Bridgeland, & Diiulio (2009, p. 7).

So, what is the antidote for this talent erosion among minority students? At least part of it must be learning experiences that raise expectations and challenge and engage students.

In 1988, The Jacob Javits Gifted and Talented Students Education Act (Javits) was passed to support gifted education. (At the time of this writing, Javits focuses on research and strategies to develop the inclusion of socioeconomically disadvantaged students and minority, disabled, or English language learners in gifted programs where the participation of these groups has been limited in the past.) A number of programs funded by Javits have used advanced curriculum for all students, including those in the minority groups, to successfully increase learning and performance. A report on the Javits-funded "Project Breakthrough" in economically depressed South Carolina districts concluded:

> Change in teaching created a change in learning as evidenced by . . . significant achievement gains. Results suggest that, even with minimal curricular intervention, minority and low-income students benefit from advanced curricula and instructional strategies that challenge them. (Swanson, 2006, p. 11)

Swanson concluded that this approach "created a rich broth of curricular experiences so that unidentified gifted students would 'bubble up' to the top" (2006, p. 12). Once again we are looking at a change in approach. Instead of viewing students through the lens of their deficits (e.g., not proficient in English, not proficient in writing, not a good speller) and applying drill-and-kill methodology to "fix" these deficits, we can approach them from another angle. We can provide all students—even if they have yet to master the English language—with full access to problem-solving, hands-on, content-rich learning opportunities. Through these opportunities, they will have the chance to access and demonstrate hidden talents that will affect their overall achievement in a positive direction.

Understanding how to identify giftedness will equip you to recommend Spanish-speaking (and other) students for participation in special programs in your district. But without some knowledge of this subject, student abilities can easily remain unseen or masked by the evidence of lower English proficiency in some areas. The following pages provide a review for teachers who need more information on the characteristics and behaviors of advanced students.

What Is "Gifted" Anyway?

When you think of bright or gifted students, does an image of the high-achiever that produces outstanding work flash into your

---

In a 2007 study, researchers at the University of Virginia found the following:

- More than 33 percent of teachers do not believe that the potential for academic giftedness is found in all socioeconomic groups.
- More than 78 percent of teachers do believe that the potential for academic giftedness is found in all racial and ethnic groups.
- Teachers focused on recommending remediation for deficits before suggesting enrichment, acceleration, or other ways of capitalizing on a child's strengths.
- Some 75 percent of teachers had difficulty believing that a child with limited vocabulary could be considered gifted.
- A recent meta-analysis showed that teachers were less likely to refer African American and Latino or Latina students for gifted programs than white students, with a difference of almost one full standard deviation.

Sources: Little and Kaesberg (2011, p. 10) and Brighton, Moon, Jarvis, and Hockett (2007, pp. 155–175).

mind? This type of student, demonstrating advanced intellectual ability and high production capacity, can certainly be gifted. But who are we overlooking if this is our only concept of an intelligent student?

Giftedness is a broad, multifaceted concept and hard to define. We have traditionally used IQ tests to measure it, but as you know, giftedness is not necessarily quantitative. In fact, when we do define it quantitatively based on test scores, we often overlook the highly creative students who most need our help and advocacy. It is an art, not a science, to truly understand and identify giftedness.

> Gifted is not a matter of degree but a different quality of experiencing: vivid, absorbing, penetrating, encompassing, complex, commanding—a way of being quiveringly alive.
>
> —M. Piechowski (Willis, 2009, p. 15)

Within the range of gifted people, there are different intensities and types of giftedness. You do not have to be an Einstein to be gifted, nor do you have to be a musical prodigy. You do not have to be fluent in English. This is the federal government's definition:

> The term *gifted and talented student* means children and youths who give evidence of higher performance capability in such areas as intellectual, creative, artistic, or leadership capacity, or in specific academic fields, and who require services or activities not ordinarily provided by the schools in order to develop such capabilities fully. Outstanding talents are present in children and youth from all cultural groups, across all economic strata, and in all areas of human endeavor (U.S. Department of Education, 1993; National Association for Gifted Children, 2011b).

Characteristics of Gifted Individuals

Joseph Renzulli, a well-known educator in the field, has pointed out that gifted behaviors can be found "in certain people (not all people), at certain times (not all the time), and under certain circumstances (not all circumstances)" (National Association for Gifted Children, 2011b).

Teachers of ELL or minority students find it helpful to have a variety of methods for identifying gifted students. It is critically

Clark (2007) offers the following summary of characteristics that could suggest giftedness.

- A strong desire to learn
- Intense, sometimes unusual interests
- Unusual ability to communicate with words, numbers, or symbols
- Effective, often inventive strategies for recognizing and solving problems
- Exceptional ability to retain and retrieve information, resulting in a large storehouse of information
- Extensive and unusual questions, experiments, and explorations
- A quick grasp of new concepts, connections; a sense of deeper meanings
- Logical approaches to figuring out solutions
- An ability to produce many highly original ideas
- A keen, often unusual sense of humor (p. 25)

important to use multiple criteria when assessing ability and achievement in gifted Hispanic students, especially ELLs who have a linguistic barrier. Castellano (1998) suggests a combination of the following:

- Ethnographic assessment procedures (student is observed in varied contexts over time)
- Dynamic assessment (student has opportunities to transfer newly acquired skills to novel situations)
- Portfolio assessment
- Test scores in native or English language
- Teacher observations
- Behavioral checklists
- Past school performance
- Interviews with parents
- Writing samples and other samples of creativity or achievement
- Input from classmates who share similar or different cultures

Creative positives, interest inventories, parental input, Torrance Tests of Creative Thinking, and portfolios are all tools that correspond with Castellano's list of criteria. In the next sections we explore categories of high ability that teachers can observe as they seek out the gifted bilingual students in their classrooms.

Three Broad Characteristics of Giftedness

Joan Franklin Smutny (2001) proposes that teachers think about giftedness through a wide-angled lens, specifically, three broad characteristics: advanced intellectual ability, high degree of creativity, and heightened sensibilities. This is a user-friendly concept to apply in a classroom setting.

Advanced Intellectual Ability

Children with remarkable intellectual ability are usually the students most obviously identified for gifted programs or instructional modifications at school. Academically gifted children can easily absorb, synthesize, analyze, and apply information. They may be advanced readers, have a detailed memory, quickly process new information, use logic and critical thinking in complex ways, and be curious, asking a lot of "why" and "what if" questions.

High Degree of Creativity

To some extent, creative children need advocacy the most. They have a tendency to believe something is wrong with them because they think so differently from other kids. Highly creative children often push the limits, stare off into space daydreaming, spend too much time looking for different ways to do work they find boring, doodle or draw on their papers, march to the beat of their own drummer, and want to know what comes next. Think of Sandra Cisneros (discussed in Chapter 4) and the dichotomy between her performance in fifth grade and her concurrent voracious reading and writing. If her teacher had known how to approach this student differently (e.g., "Hmm, a daydreamer; what might she be thinking?") she may have discovered her love for libraries and books, and her creative writing, much sooner.

Heightened Sensibilities

Many gifted children are extremely intense, unusually aware of their own moods and emotions, and capable of thinking and feeling deeply about many things. Sensibility is a child's capacity to be involved with something in a deep, internal way. Children with heightened sensibilities often feel everything with more depth and detail, have a close connection with all living things, and are concerned about world problems. They often have a finely tuned intuition or insight that enables them to see and feel things well beyond their years.

Questions to Ask to Determine If Students Fall Into These Categories

Usually a child falls into one of the three categories, sometimes with crossover between two areas. Rarely does a child evidence characteristics across the board. Used in conjunction with the creative positives, the series of questions in Figure 5.1 can help you determine if you have a student who would benefit from inclusion in your district's gifted program and additional enriched classroom work.

Figure 5.1   Who Falls Into These Categories?

Advanced Intellectual Ability

- Does the child tend to think logically?
- Do you find yourself surprised by the level of conversation you have with him?
- Are you struck by her ability to figure out math problems in her head?
- Can he absorb, synthesize, and analyze information easily?
- Do you wonder how she came to know the things she knows?
- Is he an advanced reader?
- Does she have a detailed memory?
- Is he exceedingly curious, asking a lot of questions, especially "why"?

High Degree of Creativity

- What does the child most love to do?
- Does she invent or modify objects to use in unusual ways?
- Does he improvise with toys or games?
- Does she push the limits?
- Are his papers filled with doodles and sketches?
- Does she spend (too much!) time looking for different ways to do work she finds boring?
- Is he a daydreamer?
- Does she like to be different?
- Does he have a vivid imagination?
- Is she happiest when she is free to follow her own thoughts and form her own conclusions?

Heightened Sensitivities

- Does the child respond in an intensely deep or detailed way to what he sees, hears, touches, tastes, and smells?
- Is she unusually attuned to other people's feelings?
- Does he feel deeply about many things?
- Does she ask questions or express concern about world problems?
- Can he "read" people and situations?
- Is she a perfectionist?

Source: Adapted from Smutny (2001).

Importance of Early Identification

The ramifications of inadequate early intervention for talent development are likely to be most severe for students from poor and cultural minority backgrounds. High potential in these students is often masked in the primary years by a lack of school readiness following inequitable preschool and early home experiences.

Source: Brighton et al. (2007, p. vii).

Countless research has been conducted in the field of gifted education that demonstrates the need to identify talent at an early age. However, many districts do not even test for giftedness until third grade, if they use standard assessments at all. For minority and low SES students especially, this is a dangerous practice. As we noted in Chapter 4, the achievement gap widens dramatically for Latino students after first grade.

Teachers are usually the linchpins in referring young students for gifted testing or placement. However, it has been found that as many as 50 percent of teachers do not believe that students should be identified at an early age for fear of being pushed academically (Brighton et al., 2007). In fact, the converse can be much more detrimental to the children. If gifted students do not receive the proper educational interventions early in their primary careers, they are at risk of underachievement and unrealized potential.

Best practices for districts include allowing multiple criteria for entry into a gifted program (such as observation, portfolios, creativity tests, linguistically sensitive tests) and blanket testing across an entire grade level in a primary grade. Such a practice enables district programs to avoid relying too much on the teacher referral system, which is by nature subjective and wrought with inconsistencies. When all students in one grade level are evaluated with an appropriate, nonverbal test, language ability becomes less of a factor.

The Los Angeles Unified School District began to test all second graders at a number of its traditionally low-performing schools in 2009, increasing the representation of minorities in the Gifted and Talented Education (GATE) programs. In fact, in 2008 before this approach was implemented, not one student was found gifted at a particular school with 75 percent Latino enrollment. That number rose to thirteen gifted students when all second graders were evaluated.

Blanket testing provides an opportunity to increase expectations, support, and learning motivation for bright students who are at risk for underachievement. Parents are grateful for the in-class enrichment and outside experiences their children receive as part of GATE, as these greatly increase their motivation and chances for success.

Angel Bass, superintendent of instruction for the nonprofit that manages the Los Angeles Unified School District low-performing schools, said, "We've missed the fact that our children are really talented. We need to make sure our teachers know that, our parents know that and our students know they are gifted" (Blume, 2010). The benefits that can come from blanket testing can be life-changing for students who may have previously been overlooked for gifted programs due to underperformance, lower language ability, or a host of other factors. At the same time, there should be opportunities for teacher referral in the event that a child does not test well but excels in another qualifying category.

If you are a higher-level teacher, including middle school and high school, and your district has missed the window of opportunity for blanket testing, your actions still matter. Think again of Sandra Cisneros and Enrique (see Chapter 4). They needed to be recognized for their talents in order to truly understand the importance of education and to motivate them to work. If you cannot refer a student to a gifted program at these latter grades, at least offer encouraging words about a perceived talent, suggest outside resources that will help develop this talent (such as math competitions online or creative writing contests), and become a mentor. Pass this information along to other teachers that have the child in class this year, as well as to their teachers the following year, to keep the support network going. Finally, if you do find yourself a trained and certificated GATE teacher, offering and using the strategies and techniques you have been trained with will benefit all students—they do not have to be labeled GATE to receive this specialized instruction.

Gifted Characteristics of Child Interpreters

Based on extensive case studies and research, Valdés discovered that Latino children who interpret for their parents and other relatives develop the ability to react quickly to high-pressured situations. They demonstrate cognitive flexibility as they effectively broker business between English-speaking adults and their limited English proficient elders. Situations where they interpret include taking phone calls at home or summarizing television programs or ads; registering at school, acting as go-betweens in parent-teacher conferences or meetings, and translating school correspondences; communicating with health care professionals or translating documents; communicating in business settings such as banks, insurance companies, stores, and even helping parents with job interviews (Valdés, 2003).

Valdés (2003) further found that parents select children to act as interpreters based on a number of the following qualifications:

- Perceived mastery of both Spanish and English
- Attention to detail in speaking
- Pleasing disposition
- Good listening and communication skills
- Patience
- Willingness to interpret
- Ability to understand and communicate nuances of language
- Confidence, extroverted personality

I am a first-grade teacher and job share with another teacher. Last year we had a student by the name of Natalia. Her mother didn't speak any English but brought her the Friday before the first day of school to see her classroom and possibly meet her teachers. We had the pleasure of meeting her and finding out that when Natalia started kindergarten, she spoke no English at all. You wouldn't know that in speaking with the gregarious little girl. She was excited to start school on Monday and we were excited to have her.

It didn't take us long to notice that this little girl was quick to learn all concepts and eager for more. She knew her letters and sounds and was one of our more fluent readers. While she was quick at decoding words, she often had a difficult time with comprehension. She was the first to raise her hand with questions and always wanted to know what words meant or "How do you say this in English?" She appeared to have a good grasp of her native language and could help me translate things to her mother. This is often difficult for our students because they are young and, while they understand what we're saying, they can't always translate it into their first language.

We only had Natalia a short time, about two months. She and her mom had to go back to Mexico. We were sad to see her go. She is definitely a student that benefited from ELD instruction. She was bright, eager to learn, and with more English language, she would go far. Her mother would constantly tell us that "Natalia is going to have a better life than me. I want her to have more than I could have."

We missed Natalia so much. It was a wonderful surprise to see her back at our school in second grade this year. She remembered us and came up to us with her infectious smile and said to me, "Hi, Mrs. Moore! I'm back!" There is no doubt in my mind that she will learn everything she can this year and be a light to the people around her.

—Melissa, first-grade teacher

Acting as a translator in any situation involves problem-solving in which translators must devise ways of understanding and interpreting what is said (Valdés, 2003). While most adult interpreters are highly trained for the job and highly developed in at least two languages, immigrant Latino children have varying levels of proficiency in both English and Spanish.

Valdés and her team evaluated a select group of young interpreters to study their processes, performance, and accuracy by putting them through a series of simulations like those they may have encountered with their parents. The students demonstrated "high performance capacity in areas considered to be characteristic of superior general intellectual ability including memory, abstract word knowledge, and abstract reasoning" (Valdés, 2003, p. 166). Exhaustive research as part of this study and its results led Valdés to assert that the high cognitive functioning demonstrated by young interpreters falls easily within the federally recognized definition of giftedness.

> The term *gifted and talented student* means children and youths who give evidence of higher performance capability in such areas as intellectual, creative, artistic, or leadership capacity, or in specific academic fields, and who require services or activities not ordinarily provided by the schools in order to develop such capabilities fully. Outstanding talents are present in children and youth from all cultural groups, across all economic strata, and in all areas of human endeavor. (U.S. Department of Education, 1993; National Association for Gifted Children, 2011b)

Valdés argues that a child's designation as the family interpreter should be a factor in identifying giftedness. But even more than simply qualifying these talented translators for entry into gifted programs as we know them today, she asserts that the ability to interpret should be identified as a student strength and leveraged to connect the high cognitive functioning young translators demonstrate to their academic work (Valdés, 2003).

Using the federal definition as a basis, Valdés calls for an expanded concept of giftedness that includes linguistic and analytic giftedness, which is exemplified by a number of commonly-known characteristics of gifted behavior:

- Excellent memory
- Abstract and logical thinking
- Ability to store and retrieve information rapidly, accurately, and selectively
- Ability to deal with complex problems
- Adaptation to novel situations
- High performance ability in communication
- High performance ability in interpersonal relationships
- Sensitivity to feelings of others

Source: Valdés (2003).

Recommending Students for Your School's Gifted Program

If you use the tools and strategies discussed here to identify your students' talents, you likely will come across a small handful each year who may be well-served by your school's gifted program. The first step to take is to learn about the referral process in place in your district. Then, figure out what you can do to advocate for your students and get them the services that will best meet their needs. If your district does not have a gifted program, take a look at Chapter 8 for ideas on programs best suited for your students.

Potential Roadblocks and Issues

Unfortunately, it is all too easy to identify the numerous roadblocks and issues that can surface in the context of gifted and talented education. It seems to be an ongoing battle of debunking myths and misconceptions about the education of the gifted and talented student. Each of these issues is briefly addressed below.

1. **Others are opposed to "giftedness."** The National Association for Gifted Children holds that "all children deserve the highest quality of instruction possible and that such instruction will only occur when teachers are aware of and able to respond to the unique qualities and characteristics of the students they instruct" (National Association for Gifted Children, 2008). Gifted students, regardless of their primary language, need to be taught at their appropriate instructional levels. Vygotsky refers to this as a student's zone of proximal development (ZPD) (Moll, 1990).

For each child, this zone is different and each child moves at a different pace. It represents for each individual that zone in which the learning is most appropriate—not too easy, yet not too difficult—where real learning takes place. Part of determining appropriate instructional strategies for students involves investigating their individual strengths and weaknesses. This process inevitably includes looking at a child's potential areas of giftedness. To ignore a student's gifts would be to neglect their ZPD.

2. **Parents do not want their children labeled.** Parents usually only feel this way if they do not understand what it means to be identified as gifted and talented. Therefore, it is up to educators to inform and educate parents. Ultimately, parents have the final say. If they feel strongly about not having their child identified and labeled as such,

then educators must respect their wishes, though they can and should continue to provide enrichment and differentiate the curriculum as needed.

3. Parents hold misconceptions about what being gifted and talented means. We all come from different educational experiences. Despite the volumes of research on gifted and talented programs and students, there is no singular universal definition for the term. However, many experts do agree on certain components of a gifted program, as well as on certain characteristics and behaviors of gifted students. Each district needs to clarify for its educators, students, and parents what gifted and talented means. Nobody should be left guessing what is meant by this term.

4. Educators hold misconceptions about what being gifted and talented means. According to the U.S. Department of Education's *Marland Report* (Marland, 1972):

> Gifted and talented children are those identified by professionally qualified persons who by virtue of outstanding abilities are capable of high performance. These are children who require differentiated educational programs and/or services beyond those normally provided by the regular school program in order to realize their contributions to self and society.
>
> Children capable of high performance include those with demonstrated achievement and/or potential ability in any of the following areas:
>
> 1. General intellectual ability
> 2. Specific academic aptitude
> 3. Creative or productive thinking
> 4. Leadership ability
> 5. Visual and performing arts
> 6. Psychomotor ability (pp. 20–21)

This definition of gifted and talented is quite broad. Individual districts and county offices must narrow their own definitions and decide what it is they are looking for in students. This should then shape the qualification process.

5. There is a lack of professional development for educators and therefore no appropriate services to offer. The most important way to provide gifted and talented students with the education they need and deserve is by providing training for educators. Professional development in the area of gifted education can be found in numerous places. Start by contacting your school district to inquire about the services they offer. See if anyone employed is certified and qualified to offer this training. Seek out nearby school districts for the same training opportunities. Beyond your school district, you can contact your county office of education. If you are still unsuccessful in seeking out professional development in gifted education, contact your local affiliate of a state or national organization that supports gifted education, such as the Illinois Association for Gifted Children (IAGC) and the National Association for Gifted Children (NAGC). Many universities also offer courses and GATE certificates, and they usually offer classes for teachers in the evenings, weekends, and online.

6. **The mind-set in many schools is to "treat *all* students as gifted and talented."** Nicholas Colangelo, director and cofounder of the Connie Belin & Jacqueline N. Blank International Center for Gifted Education and Talent Development at the University of Iowa, states:

> If by the phrase "all children are gifted" it is meant that all children are of value, all can do more if encouraged, and all have untapped potential, I am in your camp. But if the phrase means that all kids can do calculus in sixth grade, all students can achieve a composite score of 32 on the ACT, all kids can score 780 on the SAT-M, that all students can be piano virtuosi, or play professional baseball, then I am gone from the group. (Delisle & Galbraith, 2002, p. 30)

7. **The current priority of school districts is to implement response to intervention (RtI) to meet the needs of the lower academic performers.**

> Other than ramping up professional development to improve the education of English-language learners, some school districts have focused on improving the quality of instruction through response to intervention, an approach that focuses on screening students to identify academic weaknesses and implementing a series of gradually intensifying, focused interventions to address those gaps. The Chula Vista Elementary School District, in San Diego, is considered a model in making response to intervention work for ELLs. ("English-language learners," 2011)

Much of the focus in education is on lower-performing students. The legislation of No Child Left Behind (NCLB) by Congress in 2002 has forced school districts to improve, enhance, and target education for the lowest performing students (many of whom are English language learners) in an effort to "close the achievement gap." This stringent enforcement has left the gifted and talented population at the top of this achievement gap to flounder. It has emphasized deficit-correction-based thinking and "teaching to the test," while constraining teachers to focus less on outside resources and proven methods of instruction. Most districts' RtI models of instruction ignore the top rung of students—those who are the gifted and talented, whether or not they are ELLs.

With the majority of funding being allocated to Title I school districts and program improvement schools and districts, the integral effort of administrators, legislators, and educators is to address those students performing at the lower end of the spectrum. The hope/belief/myth that the gifted and talented students will "do just fine," is one that needs to be debunked immediately! Given the lack of federal and state funding, it is up to individual teachers, administrators, and parents to educate these students at a level commensurate with their abilities. They need to be included in the RtI model as well.

8. **There is a misconception that English language learners do not fit into gifted programs and that teachers can only instruct students literate in English.** Educators need to address this issue, however controversial it may be. Consider the following analogy, if you will.

When farmers' crops receive less rain due to the natural effects of weather, they respond immediately and appropriately to ensure quality crops. Would it not follow that teachers would respond immediately and appropriately to students receiving less of an education than other students? What does it matter that farmers are dealing with a crop of carrots or strawberries?

9. **There is a misconception that gifted programs are for the "haves," not the "have nots."** One administrator has personally experienced a paradigm shift in this belief. Formerly a principal of two low-performing, low-socioeconomic elementary schools with the highest population of Spanish-speaking students in the district, she always considered gifted programs as designed for the haves, not the have nots. In other words, placing any emphasis on gifted education, training for teachers, or identification of students did not occur to her because she felt this type of programming only existed in schools with fewer ELLs and higher test scores.

Two years into her assignment as coordinator of curriculum, which included GATE Program responsibilities, she discovered that the opposite is the case. In fact, through exposure to the professional development offered at California Association for the Gifted (CAG) conferences and institutes, she now advocates for this training for *all* teachers, whether or not they have identified GATE students in their classrooms. She has experienced the training herself and has come to the conclusion that it offers good teaching practices for *all* students! An ELL herself, she acknowledges how important and powerful GATE instructional strategies could be for the ELL population.

Yes, districts can choose to offer this type of instruction just for their gifted students. And yes, there are many strategies that may only work best with gifted students. But the general concept of these techniques is to make students, gifted or not, think critically, engage in metacognition, dig deeper, explore topics more thoroughly, and further develop their abilities and interests. How can that be wrong for any student?

Review

Now that you have more information about giftedness and how to identify your ELL and Latino students for inclusion in gifted programs from an early age, we hope that you take action in doing so. In the next chapter, we explore the importance, as in Enrique's case, of parent involvement and how you as a classroom teacher can facilitate this.

Thinking Questions

1. Consider your students, past and present. Select one or two underachievers or low performers who strike you as creative. Answer the questions in Figure 5.1 to determine which categories of giftedness apply to your student(s). With your 20-20 hindsight, would you recommend that student for a gifted program?

2. Do you know any students who translate for their parents? Do you see the characteristics used by parents to select their young translators manifested in the classroom?

Night covers the sky
The touch of the devil
chills the earth
He opens the earth
Out come his minions
dancing with excitement

But soon . . .
a bell rings
Light is shed upon the earth
the sun rising
the devil dying

Harps play softly
people sing
as the devil and his minions
return
leaving the earth
untouched

—Analissa, Grade 9

6

Effective Ways for Teachers to Connect With Spanish-Speaking Parents

If we were to ask educators why they originally became teachers, most responses would include a love for children and a desire to help them. Rarely do we meet an educator whose sole motive was to interact with the parents of students. Nonetheless, educators, whether they are teachers, principals, counselors, or psychologists, need to view parents as key players in educating children. In this chapter, you will find ways to enhance the teacher-parent-student relationships to build on the success of the students in your own classroom, school, and district.

> We propose that your major goal in parenting for high potential is to help your child develop into a healthy (in many ways) and effective person who is an independent learner and a creatively productive person.
> —Nancy A. Cook, Carol V. Wittig, Donald J. Treffinger
> (2011, p. 243)

Granted, what this looks like in different homes varies, but embracing such an objective is a great way to begin working with parents of gifted students, or *all* students for that matter. This sharing of knowledge provides the foundation of a successful educational experience. A shared and known goal will help the larger group to progress farther and faster.

Bright Hispanic Students Need an Advocate

In fifth grade, Ramón, a second-generation Hispanic American, tested in the highest percentile on every subject for his state assessments. He was placed in the advanced track throughout sixth grade and received straight As. On his state tests in sixth grade, Ramón tested below average in all subjects. Because of his sixth-grade test results, he was then placed in both remedial math and English for his seventh-grade year. Ramón's mother did not understand the educational system and did not know what to do. Fortunately, Ramón had a cousin in college who had successfully navigated the district's school system a few years before. She became his advocate, meeting with the junior high school's assistant principal to point out the inconsistencies in Ramón's placement and requesting that he be moved to a level commensurate with his stellar sixth-grade school performance.

Daniela is a joyful, loving seventh grader who responds well to authority. She does not have a problem listening to or following directions. She was born in the United States, and her single mother, who works hard to put food on the table and does not get paid time off from her job, speaks only Spanish.

Daniela is doing poorly in school and has been given an Individualized Education Plan (IEP) under a specific learning disability (SLD) diagnosis. Her mother wants the best for her daughter and wants her to do well in school. She has come to a number of IEP meetings and, even though there has always been an interpreter present, she has never left with a clear understanding of what the problems are or what can be done to fix them.

Teachers say Daniela only pays attention in class 70 percent of the time. They report that she drifts off the rest of the time. At one point, the school found a tutor for Daniela. The tutor was late to sessions and eventually did not show up, so the family gave up on the tutor.

(Continued)

As a family friend, I became concerned about Daniela and her mother's frustration in not being able to understand the problems or the solutions. I began to study her documents and talk with the school. I also did my own research. After administering an interest inventory to Daniela, it was apparent that she had many interests and a desire to learn. She expressed interest in art and science and studying animals, and she said she would like to become a veterinarian. She also loves reading books that relate to films.

The short of it is that Daniela wants to learn, but for some reason is having a problem and it just keeps getting worse. She continues to be in English as a second language (ESL) classes, even though she has undergone all of her schooling in the U.S. In fact, the lowest grade on her report card was a D in ESL. Nothing really is being done to fix the problem, even though she has a willing parent who wants the best for her and tries as hard as she can to get information.

—Anna M., attorney and special education advocate

Retired assistant superintendent and gifted education specialist, Dr. Carolyn Cooper, states, "A non-negotiable of serving advanced-level students is explaining to *all* constituents—and to gifted students' parents, especially—the *purpose* of gifted education services" (2008, p. 11). Educators need to connect with parents of their gifted students, whether ELL or not. Dr. Cooper clarifies the type of help parents of gifted students need in two parts:

First, the school must know which issues concern parents of gifted students most. . . . The second kind of parent assistance needed is a targeted education. Instead of expecting them to know all about giftedness . . . we need to educate them about these critical areas affecting their gifted children. (p. 10)

Understanding what the parents of gifted students need to know and addressing up front the issues that concern them can facilitate two-way communication between the school and parents. The benefits of parent involvement are clear: a growing body of research shows that successful parent involvement improves not only student behavior and attendance but also positively affects student achievement.

Teachers and administrators must step back and take a look at what goes on in their classrooms, schools, and school districts. Sometimes, it is easy to lose sight of the bigger picture and neglect to acknowledge

Academic Inhibitors

- Teacher delays identification of the student as a gifted learner until the child can speak fluent English.
- The gifted student is hesitant to participate in class because the lack of English depresses performance.
- The gifted student feels like an academic failure.
- Educators perceive limited English ability as synonymous with limited academic abilities.
- *Parents are not informed about the dimensions of giftedness* [emphasis added].

Source: California Association for the Gifted (1999).

that parents need to be participants in their children's education just as much as teachers are. Schools often fail to engage parents because they do not think they can. "A lot of it is perception. Teachers perceive that families don't want to be involved when, in fact, families don't know how to be involved," says Karen Salinas, communications director for the Center on School, Family, and Community Partnerships at Johns Hopkins University, as quoted in the newsletter of the Center for Comprehensive School Reform and Improvement (2005).

Advocating for Gifted English Language Learners: An Activity Handbook for Professional Development and Self-Study is published by the California Association for the Gifted (CAG) (1999) in both English and Spanish. This publication outlines five specific academic inhibitors that affect students who are learning English and striving to be recognized as gifted learners. Key to this list is the connection schools must make with the student's parents.

Establishing a Team: Parent, Teacher, and Student

In her book, *Why Bright Kids Get Poor Grades and What You Can Do About It*, Dr. Sylvia Rimm (2008) outlines certain laws of achievement, or rather, steadfast reasons why students choose or choose *not* to achieve. Rated number one on her list is that children are more likely to be achievers if their parents join together to give the same clear and positive message about school effort and expectations. If parents are expected to be a part of the team, then they need to know what the classroom teacher is doing in order to play a supportive role in the home. Communication with parents is a key ingredient to maintaining a successful functioning classroom, regardless of the student's primary language.

The benefits of meaningful parental involvement in the education of children are widely documented. Student achievement and graduation rates increase (Henderson & Berla, 1995), and families gain self-sufficiency with greater understanding and confidence in the American education and social service systems (Bermudez & Marquez, 1996; Mardirosian & Ochoa, 1996). School quality also improves with parents volunteering as tutors and activity organizers, as well as participants in school governance and advocacy. (Gallagher, 2007)

Even in a district with many Spanish-speaking parents, this is possible. Bilingual educators and parents can step in as interpreters to validate their participation in meetings.

Something radically changes when a bridge of communication is built that connects a parent to his student's learning experience at school. These moments can be life-altering, forever revolutionizing the way the family looks at, treats, and reveres the child's education. Educators may already have a personal knowledge of this parent-teacher connection in their repertoire and take this knowledge for granted. Additionally, educators who have school-age children of their own tend to take more initiative in opening up the lines of communication with teachers. Parents who are not educators do not necessarily have access to this background knowledge.

Yes, currently, the demands on teachers are at an all-time high—classrooms are crowded, jobs are in jeopardy, financial support is scarce, curriculum materials are old. Nevertheless, the fundamental responsibilities of a teacher have not changed. Teachers can take small steps to keep communication open and constant with families by making five phone calls home each day until the class list is complete, visiting one home each month, and sending notes, checklists, or updates to parents on a weekly basis, in an effort to reach out to them.

Classroom teachers need not hold back, regardless of language barriers that may exist. They can find out who might translate in their district or at their site if they cannot communicate directly with the students' parents. Teachers also can find someone to make phone calls for them in the home language of their students. There is no way to rewind time and fix miscommunication or communication that never happened. Do it right

> Educators say that what they want from parents is:
>
> • To be appreciated;
> • To be respected;
> • To be trusted;
> • To be given consideration;
> • To be understood; and
> • To hear positives.
>
> This list mirrors what parents say they expect from educators!
>
> —Arlene R. DeVries (2011, pp. 316–317)

from the start. A teacher's connection with students' parents should take precedence over the fears or misconceptions that exist due to language barriers.

Below are some easy ways teachers can initiate communication with parents:

- Send a letter home to students on the class roster(s) a few weeks before the school year begins. Tell them about yourself. Mention the supplies students will need to be successful in your class. Include a list of ways parents can assist in and out of the classroom (refer to Chapter 3 for specifics). Be sure that these letters are translated and printed in the predominant language(s) in your school.
- In an introduction letter to students and their parents, invite them both into the classroom early on the first day of school. Serve hot cocoa and coffee. This kind yet simple gesture will help get the year started on the right foot. Parents will know right away that your classroom is inviting and welcoming.
- Contact the parents of all students within the first few weeks of school and personally invite them to Back-to-School Night. As a time-saving alternative, make and send home computer generated invitations to this event. Follow up with a photocopied thank-you note.
- Offer extra credit to those students who attend evening events with their parents as an incentive to draw a larger audience.
- Make at least three phone calls home a day. Share a compliment on the student's behalf with the parent. Should you need to make a not-so-positive call later in the year, this will not be your first contact with a student's parents.

Once the parents of every student on the roster have been contacted, the makings of a team have been established—teacher, student, and parent—working together to achieve success.

To bring the students on as part of this team, the teacher can administer a general interest survey or inventory to draw them in and to discover who the students really are. The interest survey found in Jim Delisle and Judy Galbraith's book *When Gifted Kids Don't Have All the Answers* (2002) is quite useful as it not only asks students to examine themselves as learners, but to share their perceptions about being identified as gifted learners.

While the book targets gifted students, the survey can be used with all students with minor editing. The results of this survey also help the teacher know how to differentiate the curriculum and appeal to individual interests.

Another great resource to use for this purpose is an interest inventory. Diane Heacox (2002) has an excellent inventory in her book, *Differentiating Instruction in the Regular Classroom: How to Reach and Teach All Learners, Grades 3–12*. This particular inventory addresses all learners. It asks interesting questions that intrigue most students so much that they want to share their thoughts, feelings, preferences, and interests.

Yet another great resource, an interest inventory, can be found in Susan Winebrenner's book, *Teaching Gifted Kids in the Regular Classroom: Strategies and Techniques Every Teacher Can Use to Meet the Academic Needs of the Gifted and Talented* (2001).

Questionnaires and inventories such as these can be completed with lower-elementary students, but in an interview format. At the end of such questionnaires, ask students to mark if they prefer to have letters addressed to their own parents in Spanish or English. This will save the teacher time and money, rather than providing everything in both Spanish and English. Parents will appreciate the efforts of the teacher to accommodate their preferences.

Explaining Giftedness and Gifted Education to Parents

A first important step in communicating with Spanish-speaking parents of gifted children is to inform them about what it means to be gifted. The acronyms that school districts use, including GATE (Gifted and Talented Education), TAG (Talented and Gifted), and GT (gifted and talented), do not directly translate into Spanish. And think about the English-speaking parents who have never heard of a TAG program. Both sets of parents need the same background information in order to understand what this means for their children. Begin with this goal in mind: you want parents and students to understand the implications of being gifted so that they can succeed in school and obtain the appropriate support.

Nevertheless, the concept and purpose of gifted education is difficult for some parents to grasp. If the parents lack an extensive educational background themselves, they may not have encountered the concept of gifted education. Occasionally, parents do question why their children are in a gifted program, and why they should prefer this over a general educational placement.

> Being GATE has been an amazing experience. It has given me the tools to be a successful person in life. Thanks to the learning experience GATE has provided me with I am now graduating a year early. I have also learned that my learning capabilities go beyond those of the other students because . . . I am different . . . I am GATE.
>
> —Mariana, Hispanic GATE student, twelfth grade

Educators, teachers, and administrators should tread lightly when explaining the value of gifted education for someone else's child. Avoid being influential or opinionated. Present the facts. Whenever possible, share commentary about a student's particular characteristics, gifts, and learning styles in an effort to show how the gifted classroom will best meet his or her educational needs. Parents always appreciate knowing what extra training gifted education teachers receive in order to address the students' unique needs. In addition, you can include a variety of personal testimonies of those students who have been enrolled in your gifted program.

Hosting Successful Parent Meetings

> Studies have revealed that 75 to 80 percent of students feel that parental support is important to their school success.
> —Joyce Van Tassel-Baska, educator (2009, p. 27)

Parent meetings are opportune times to build on the strength of the parent-teacher-student team. If done right, and with extra care, these meetings can be more successful than imagined. To ensure that parent meetings are successful, consider the following suggestions.

- Organize the structure, agenda, and speakers for your meeting at least one month in advance.
- Send home a save-the-date notice with the students at least two weeks in advance (be sure to include translations of this information as well).
- Include on this notice the following details:
  - Date, time, location of meeting
  - Items to be sold at the meeting—that way parents can plan ahead to bring money
  - Topic of the meeting
  - Child care or enrichment options for students—that way parents will know whether to bring their children

- Send a second reminder via an automated telephone service, like ConnectEd (messages can be recorded in any language).
- Connect the meeting topic to the future academic success of the children and parents certainly will want to attend.
- Be sure that this is a meeting you yourself would want to attend. If not, reorganize, restructure, and begin planning.
- Provide all handouts in the languages the parents speak (if possible).
- Include a door prize drawing at every meeting in which educational items or school program items are awarded (e.g., bumper stickers, pencils, T-shirts, sweatshirts, educational games, enriching books for all ages, donated gift certificates to local businesses).
- Sell organization clothing and items before and after meetings. This is a great opportunity to get items sold, to make some money, and to show pride in the program.
- Try to keep the meeting time to one hour or less if possible. Especially on school nights, parents will be eager to return home and will be more likely to attend future meetings if they know you respect their time.
- Offer child care or enrichment activities for children while the parents meet. Contact local agencies, high schools, organizations, clubs, and community service programs to assist with this offering.
- Build a lending library of valuable parenting and gifted resources that parents can check out from meeting to meeting.
- Allow time for parents to share some of their own experiences related to the meeting topic. This practice is encouraging because parents get to hear that others are experiencing the same situations.
- Include time for parents to brainstorm topics that interest them.
- Congratulate the parents for taking such an active role in their children's education just by attending the meeting!

Meetings can focus on topics that the parents have requested. However, it is beneficial to everyone to cover the following topics year after year.

- How to help my child with homework when I do not get it
- What it means to have a child who is gifted

- What resources are out there for my gifted child (see the appendix)
- How to parent a gifted child with a nongifted sibling
- How to manage the behavior and misbehavior of a gifted child
- How to ease the transition from elementary to junior high school
- Enriching your child's mathematics or language arts curriculum
- Advocating for your child's education
- Learning about the gifted child who is creative
- Meeting the social and emotional needs of gifted children
- Brain research behind giftedness

One way to access resources for these meeting topics is to connect with an affiliate of your state's gifted association. Identify your region and contact the teacher or parent representative. Many regions offer educational meetings, informational events, and special presentations throughout the year. Often the executive board members offer presentations as part of their responsibilities in leadership.

It is very rewarding to bring a guest speaker in and watch the faces of the parents as they experience those "a-ha moments," learn something new about helping their own child, and write down a website that will be educational for their family. It is rare to see parents getting this exposure and education.

Parent meetings can be organized in many ways. Those who attend may speak one, two, or even more languages. Presentations delivered in one language and then simultaneously interpreted in a second language will inevitably extend the meeting time. One portion of the audience will not be listening to at least half of the presentation. With all of these factors considered, think about three different format suggestions for successful parent meetings.

So many times, during our district GATE parent meetings, I take a moment to reflect and look around the room. I see parents who just got off of work, mothers rocking babies to sleep, students sitting quietly reading their favorite books, parents who work in the fields exhausted and weather-beaten, fathers taking notes. Anywhere from 150 to 250 parents crowd our board room, some opting to stand against the walls. They feel invited. They know we love their children. They want to know how they can help and be involved. The best part is watching the guest speaker's eyes widen as the parents flood into the room filling chairs. They never believe us when we tell them how many parents attend. I cannot help but fight back the tears; I am awestruck every time.

—Gina, teacher on special assignment for GATE, coauthor

Format 1: This format is designed for large audiences of both English- and Spanish-speaking parents. It allows presenters to address *all* parents in English *and* Spanish at the same time, but in two different rooms. In one room the first presenter speaks in English and in the other room the second presenter speaks in Spanish. Halfway through the meeting, the presenters switch rooms and repeat their presentation in the other language. With bilingual presenters, you have just met the language needs of both groups and avoided the frustration of sitting through a meeting where parents only understand half of what is said. (See Figure 6.1.)

Format 2: This format is designed for a large group of parents who predominately speak English with a small group of parents who do not. Provide headsets, like the Whisper System, for the parents who do not speak English. Have an interpreter standing in the back of the room speak into the microphone that feeds all of the parents' headsets. It is crucial that the interpreter have background knowledge of the topic being discussed so that he or she will know the vocabulary well. The presenter will not be taking cues from this interpreter to slow down so she or he must work quickly. This format gives parents who do not speak English the opportunity to learn about the program, but may be more challenging for parents of English language learners to ask questions or share concerns. The main advantage is that this format cuts the meeting time in half by providing the presentation in both languages simultaneously. (See Figure 6.1.)

Format 3: This format is promising for settings in which large numbers attend and the primary language of parents is nearly split down the middle. This format is ideal also if the meeting space is too small for the large turnout. It offers two separate meeting times based on the language needs of families. By splitting the entire parent population in half, student attendance will be more manageable as well. Having too many students in child-care, or even enrichment, can raise numerous concerns among parents. (See Figure 6.1.)

When selecting presenters for parent meetings, be sure to inform them of the particular format and about the possibility of providing information in Spanish. Having a "copresenter/interpreter" can be tricky; some presenters may not feel comfortable in this setting. Either way, one of the three formats discussed should meet your district's needs if you have a large population of second-language speakers.

Regardless of the meeting topic, the format, or the guest speaker, one factor will be key to the success of your parent meetings. Whether you are the director of curriculum, the coordinator, a classroom

Figure 6.1 Sample Parent Meeting Formats

Format 1	*Rooms needed: two*
6:00–6:20	Welcome! Announcements in both languages. Share format of the meeting in Room A.
6:20–6:25	Spanish-speaking parents move to adjacent Room B. English-speaking parents stay in Room A.
6:25–6:45	Speaker A gives the presentation in Room A in English. Speaker B gives the presentation in Room B in Spanish.
6:45–7:05	Speaker A moves to Room B to give the presentation in Spanish. Speaker B moves to Room A to give the presentation in English.
7:05–7:10	All parents reconvene in Room A.
7:10–7:30	Closing remarks in both English and Spanish. Q & A. Thank parents for coming. Prizes: Educational materials.

Format 2	*Rooms needed: one large room (all parents in one room)*
6:00–6:10	Welcome! Announcements in English. Have the interpreter near the back to avoid distractions. Provide headphones for the non-English-speaking parents.
6:10–7:00	Presentation in English. Interpreter simultaneously provides information in Spanish via the headsets.
7:00–7:15	Closing remarks in English. Interpreter to provide these in Spanish. Q & A in English/Spanish (with interpreter). Thank parents for coming. Prizes: Educational materials.

Format 3	*Rooms needed: one*
6:00–6:45	Entire meeting in English.
6:45–7:00	Q & A in English. Closing remarks. Prizes: Educational materials.
7:00–7:45	Entire meeting in Spanish.
7:45–8:00	Q & A in Spanish. Closing remarks. Prizes: Educational materials.

teacher, or even the superintendent, you need to step off the stage and get out in the audience. Meet the families, greet them, try your best to at least say a few words in their primary language, ask how their children are, and inquire about the schools they attend. Get out there and mix in. Do not just stand up on the stage waiting for everyone to file in and then begin the meeting. No personal connection can be fostered in this way; parents will not feel that you have connected with them. This simple yet critical move will make families feel so welcome that they will want to come back. Shaking hands, learning names, and making connections to families is a must!

Staying in Touch With Parents About Their Children's Progress

Always keep parents informed and updated! Rare and unique is the parent who does not appreciate a note or a phone call from a teacher. Establishing a system will help make it second nature. You will want to update parents on your current projects, goals, and needs, as well as the child's progress, improvement, strengths, and weaknesses. If you do not identify your needs, parents are less able to support you (Smutny, Walker, & Meckstroth, 1997). A generic communication form is helpful in serving this purpose. Such a form, sent home to parents at the end of each week or bimonthly, might include some or all of the following elements.

- An update on curricular topics. This will enable parents to engage in conversations with their children about what they are currently learning in the classroom.
- A sneak peek at what comes next. This will enable parents to collect any materials or supplies their child may need in upcoming weeks.
- An update on the child's academic progress. This will ensure that there will be no surprises when official report cards are sent home.
- An update on the child's social or behavioral progress. Some parents may be more concerned with this than their child's academic progress.
- An update on any academic, social, or behavioral goals set by the child or the parent.
- Any personal notes from the teacher that need immediate attention from parents.

With this form, a classroom teacher can ensure that she or he is making the best effort to keep communication open and flowing with families. A consistent and familiar form makes the communication process easier for the teacher and parents. All parties will know what to look for, where to look for it (child's backpack or homework calendar), and what to write on it. To best facilitate this communication with Spanish-speaking parents, having forms in a checklist format and back-to-back in Spanish and English is a must. This will ensure that all parties are communicating the same message through their primary language.

A good practice for districts is to share templates for such forms with teachers. Districts can provide outlines and forms through their websites. A great resource for such items is Susan Winebrenner's book, *Teaching Gifted Kids in the Regular Classroom* (2001). This book provides a wide range of teacher-friendly forms to use with students and parents.

Differentiating the curriculum to match a student's academic interests and needs is of critical importance, and parents can play a supportive role if they are informed of these ongoing adjustments. With gifted children it is highly recommended that teachers offer pretesting in academic areas where these students may excel. If they show mastery before the content is even taught, then they can go on to another project or assignment. Another strategy is to have students begin working at the end of an assignment to assess level of mastery, rather than starting at the beginning. This works especially well in mathematics where the more difficult problems are last. If a gifted student can do these last problems without correction, she should not need the practice of the easier ones. Implementing these simple, minor changes in the classroom curriculum becomes easier when teachers have parents who can supervise and assist students in the home. For this to work, however, teachers need to communicate regularly and keep parents current on their children's progress.

Working With Overburdened and Resistant Parents

It is inevitable that during a career as an educator one will, more than once, meet children who come from homes with unconcerned, overburdened, uninterested, resistant, abusive, or unavailable parents. In these situations educators must be more than teachers or administrators for these students. This is part of the unwritten job description of an educator. Teachers constantly take their students' burdens to heart and take them into consideration when grading assignments. Teachers are human, but so are the students and their parents.

When faced with difficult family situations, the responsibility of the educator is twofold. First, to nurture the child, and second, to then try to make a connection with parents. Jean Sunde Peterson, PhD, professor and director of school counselor preparation at Purdue University, is a former gifted education teacher. From her extensive research and counseling experience with gifted youth and their families she made the following observations.

> Bright and talented children can be given too much deferential treatment. Parents, awed by their gifted child's adult-like wisdom, might even rely on the child to make major family decisions. Young gifted children may assume heavy household responsibilities—because they are so capable. In some situations, parents behave as if their children were their peers, confidants, or even parents. Although the children may seem to function well in these roles, not being able to trust adults to be reliable, competent, and adult-like during stressful times may contribute to insecurity. Parents can forget that adult-like children still need comfort, nurturing, and guidance. When parents assume appropriate parental roles, children are free to act their age, feel secure, and eventually move comfortably into adulthood. (2011, p. 530)

To a certain degree, nearly every parent feels overburdened. A colleague put it best when she spoke directly from the heart, telling parents firmly but gently, "I know you are tired when you get home from working all day. I know that you just want some peace and quiet. But your children need you. And when they constantly ask question after question after question, you need to listen to them, provide answers, and when you do not have the answers, encourage their natural curiosity. Whatever you do, do *not* quiet them. *Encourage* them—tell them to keep asking! Do not ignore them and do not tell them to be quiet. If they are asking, they want to know more! Celebrate that! Worry when they *are* quiet!"

To create a successful and nurturing relationship with students' families, especially those who come across as disinterested or resistant, try to see and understand their world—what their daily life is like, what their jobs entail, what they value most. In other words, find

I will never forget the parent conference I had with Tomás's mother. He refused to complete any work in class or at home. He was not disruptive except for the fact that other students observed him *not* working every day. With failing grades and chronic detention for making up work, I was anxious to meet his mother with the hopes of fixing something together.

To my surprise, Tomás's mother was in tears within just two minutes of beginning the conference—and quite obviously angry with me.

I learned something about Tomás and his family that day that transformed my outlook on him, and numerous students I taught thereafter. Tomás's father had been in and out of jail for years. Tomás lived only for the days when his father returned home after being released from jail each time. Unresponsive to his mother, she too was at a loss about what to do.

It became crystal clear to me why this particular parent felt so overburdened and appeared to be disinterested in her son's education. She was overwhelmed with her life situation and did not know what to do about it.

—Sue, seventh-grade teacher

out *why* they are so overburdened and cannot take an active role in their own children's education. The situation of some parents may be drastically different from the teacher's own condition in life, and knowing this will help educators to reach out in ways that meet their needs and concerns.

Teachers cannot expect their students' parents to show up on the school's terms, to be involved, to sit every night with their children as they complete homework, and to read to them. Parents have to be met on their own terms sometimes. If they work late, then meetings should be offered later in the evening when they can attend. If they speak a language other than English, then an interpreter should be provided. If educators speak even the slightest bit of the parents' primary language, they should attempt to speak it in conversation with them. Crossing this linguistic boundary is difficult, challenging, and often embarrassing, but educators cannot sit back and expect their students' parents to take this risk alone.

Yes, there still will be those uninvolved, unreachable parents who never make it to conferences or open house, the spring band concert, or a PTA meeting. They do exist, and they come from all socioeconomic, ethnic, and linguistic backgrounds. Educators need to do their part for the children of these parents too, whatever their level of involvement. However, teachers still can do a lot to increase parental involvement, even in the most difficult cases.

The research of educator Luis Moll focuses on what he terms, "funds of knowledge." These represent theoretical wells to tap into. They may represent the talents of students' parents, the careers and jobs parents have, the struggles that students' families experience, the cultural histories of students' families, and so forth. His project was to "draw on the knowledge and other resources found in local households for the development of classroom practice" (Gonzalez, Moll, &

Strategies for Working With Overburdened Parents

1. Reach out to parents through multiple phone call reminders at least two weeks in advance of meeting dates.

2. Bring parents together for meetings when it is convenient for them, not just convenient for school personnel.

3. Always offer an interpreter if there are any doubts about being able to communicate effectively.

4. Offer parents a meeting worth coming for. Put yourself in their shoes—would you take time out of your own busy schedule to come and listen to what you are offering? If not, then it is time to reevaluate your program.

5. Assure parents that you truly have their own children's best interests at heart.

6. Communicate clearly, often, and everywhere possible about meeting dates, times, and locations. Send this information home in the students' language(s). If the meeting location moves, put up signs for parents who may have missed the message. Inform teachers of meetings details so that they can remind students in the classroom as well.

> Our parent meetings used to begin at 5 p.m. Attendance was low and most parents arrived late. Now we do not begin our meetings until 7:00 p.m. for the Spanish-speaking parents. We found that, because we teach in an agricultural community, many of our parents did not get off work in the fields until sundown. With daylight savings time, we needed to consider that factor. Moving our meetings to 7:00 p.m. brought many more into attendance.
>
> —District administrator

7. Offer enrichment, not just child care, for families during parent meetings. Seek out groups in the community willing to come in and offer enrichment for an hour or two.

8. If it still seems as though the parents are not involved because they seem not to care about their children's education, then make a home visit. Meet with the family. Find out how the school can assist.

Amanti, 2005, p. 71). Through this lens, every family has something to offer.

Involving Parents in the Learning Experience

It goes without saying that parents can always be a great human resource for classroom teachers and students, no matter what the grade level. Parents can be invited to participate in a variety of ways.

Parent-teacher partnerships are important to differentiated classrooms. A parent always knows a child more deeply than a teacher possibly can. There's much for the teacher to learn from that depth of knowledge. On the other hand, a teacher knows a child in ways that a parent cannot. There's much for a parent to gain from that breadth of knowledge. Looking at a child from both parent and teacher viewpoints increases the chances of helping that child realize her full potential. The wisest teachers teach parents as well as children. They eagerly seek opportunities to learn from parents as well.

—Carol Ann Tomlinson (1999, p. 106)

Teachers can offer lessons that incorporate more cross-curricular projects in an effort to involve students' families, stories, experiences, cultural backgrounds, and artifacts.

What teachers learn from parents makes a difference in the kind of classrooms they design for children. By consulting with parents on the cultural practices, traditions and arts from their communities and the learning preferences of their children, teachers ensure that their students feel at home in the classroom. (Smutny, 2002, p. 37)

Barbara, a fifth-grade gifted and talented teacher always invites families in for an annual cultural study unit she does with her class. As part of her history and language arts curriculum, she assigns students a project on their own culture. They are to research information through the Internet and family members to discover all that they can about their family history. The culminating activity involves oral presentations that last a few days. Students can bring in artifacts connected to their culture, family members with life stories and special areas of expertise, performing artists, and cultural foods to share with the class. The result is a week of exciting and eventful days filled with food, presentations, guest speakers, music, art, dance, and much more! Grandparents come in to share tales of fighting firsthand in battle, mothers bring platter after platter of food many students have never heard of, and students wear traditional garb to class or bring family genealogy albums for display. Once, a student even brought in (with permission, of course) an original Samurai sword. For this fifth-grade classroom, the cultural study unit is the most exciting time of the year, every year. When all is said and done, every student has learned about his or her own cultural background, as well as the heritages of others, and has actively engaged in multiple dimensions of learning. Easily tied to social studies, language arts, and the fine arts, this unique lesson could be integrated into any elementary or even junior high classroom with a little organization on the part of the teacher. This is an effective way to connect students to their own culture and give them ownership of their learning.

Just because parents do not speak English does not mean that they should be excluded as potential presenters. This can be a unique opportunity and growing experience for students to act as interpreters for parents while they deliver their presentations. If they feel comfortable doing so, they can open the eyes of native speakers who rarely see the advantage (rather than disadvantage) these children have. Student interpreters in the classroom are living examples of the special gifts that bilingualism confers.

Parents can be invited into the classroom to share a specific talent, hobby, or interest with students. They can demonstrate how to play the guitar; to weave, knit or crochet; to write editorials for newspapers; to train animals; to draw caricatures or paint landscapes; to manage people effectively and professionally; or to sing a particular song. Most of these can be tied to the standards in one way or another. The opportunities are as broad as are the interests and careers of your students' parents.

Another opportunity for involving parents in the classroom is to invite them in on a career day. Educators are discovering more and more that career days are extremely influential events in students' lives. Schools should try to include careers of all kinds—from those requiring graduate studies, four-year college completion, two-year degrees, and those requiring vocational training, life experience, and internships or mentorships. Most employers will allow release time during the work day for such events.

Parents also can play a key role in their children's learning by supporting independent study projects (see Chapter 7). When a child, whether or not identified as gifted, already shows mastery before beginning a unit, the teacher can assess the level of knowledge or skill and take appropriate action. Independent study projects are a common way to do this. To be successful, an independent study project should not only enhance the classroom experience for the student, but create a partnership between the teacher and parent as they clarify goals, determine the necessary steps, and agree on areas of responsibility. Parent involvement enhances the learning experience considerably and opens up a unique opportunity for parent and child to work together in an academic setting. As a partner, the parent can monitor the child's progress at home, communicate with the teacher regularly, help the child find new sources of information, collect objects and materials, network with extended family and others in the neighborhood, and offer emotional support. This kind of learning experience is a collaborative one where the teacher gains a partner in the parent, the parent becomes a guide to the child, and the child becomes inspired and energized by the independent study project.

Pointers for a Successful Career Day

- Schedule the event for just half of the school day. Volunteers are more likely to be released from their job for half of a work day rather than a full day.
- Provide all presenters with an official letter on district or school letterhead so they can ask for time off.
- Provide all presenters with a detailed schedule of the day, including options of hours to volunteer.
- Provide all presenters with a list of potential topics to cover in their presentations. (Include also a list of inappropriate topics *not* to cover.)
- Include a feedback form on which presenters can indicate whether they will need any electronic equipment for their presentation (e.g., Lumens, overhead projector, laptop, CD player).
- Recruit the student council members to fill in as escorts for guests on campus. Do not forget to let all of their teachers know they will be out of class.
- Upon their arrival, provide all presenters with a professional name tag, a campus map (with adult restrooms highlighted), a clean copy of the schedule, and a warm thank-you letter or certificate of appreciation.
- Have a healthy breakfast waiting for presenters upon their arrival. Do not forget water!

Wrap-Up

Educators and parents play important roles in leading children toward greater success in the classroom. We encourage you to take these best practices to your districts and schools. Explore ways to create more productive parent meetings. Keep parents in the know from the very beginning of the school year. Offer choice and enrichment for the students. Bring parents and students on board as part of your team for student success.

Thinking Questions

1. At your district or site TAG or GATE parent meetings, is the attendance representative of at least one third of the total population of gifted students?

2. If not, why do you think more parents are not attending? What can you do about this?

3. If you were to ask any randomly selected GATE parent from your district or site what the definition of gifted and talented means, what possible answers might you get? Is this based on information that you have given them, or do you need to supply more?

> There is more to wildlife
> than I just shared
> with you
> Penguins waddling around
> the snowy ground
> Deserts filled with prickly sharp
> cacti
> Ants crawling on a dusty
> lizard
> Koalas hugging their children
> in tall trees
> Bats hanging upside down sleeping
> Some flying
> around the sky
> Kangaroos jumping
> Eagles gliding
> through the air
> Sometimes . . .
> nature surprises
> you.
>
> —Leslie, Grade 2

7

Developing the Strengths and Talents of Hispanic ELLs

Strategies for Getting Started

Antonio could not have written that poem. This was the principal's first thought when he remembered his first years in school as a frightened, shy student, barely able to write a paragraph. How could this practically mute middle school kid emerge as a serious contender in a spoken word poetry contest two years later? What the principal did not know was that Antonio's teacher recommended him for a poetry workshop taught by poets, two of whom were Chicano. A gifted student, Antonio struggled with written composition and felt lost in the classroom. Unlike the Hispanic friends he moved around with, he was hypersensitive and withdrawn, more like their mascot than a companion.

Poetry gave him confidence and a voice—a way of expressing himself in English that felt real and exciting. Antonio said that when one of the teachers performed a poem, he felt the skin on his back prickle because he was hearing something he recognized but never

113

heard in poetry. His mother said that the words "shot out of the man like he was on fire and they were hot Spanish words mixed with cool English ones and they were poetical." She said she was moved to her bones and when she looked at her son, she knew he felt the same. Antonio's relationship to the English language changed that day. In the poems he heard, he felt words play with words like music and magnify meanings.

This is significant for gifted English language learners because they experience the intersection of two languages and cultures as a complex and sometimes unsettling process. One of their greatest needs is not only to find their place in this in-between world but to make their English language learning a process of self-discovery— not just a goal they must reach for academic success. Helping them to relate creatively to language—their own as well as English—teachers provide the support ELLs need to grapple with problems of identity, language, and meaning. A gifted Guatemalan fifth grader once told how the language he now spoke in school felt like "stolen words" and he had to hide himself behind them "like a thief." Gifted students bring a high level of sensitivity and depth to their bilingual lives, and they need learning experiences to help them not only develop their strengths but address their social-emotional issues.

One young ELL who had recently immigrated and enrolled in my school had a thirst for knowledge. He had quick strategies that would connect him to ways of learning material. As a sixth grader in my class, his math ability with computation was superior. Application was there but the language hindered that progress, so for word problems he wanted a notebook of the terms translated. We did that as a class. Because this was a bilingual classroom, it was a brilliant idea and his idea became a norm in my classroom. Still to this day we call it "the smartest sixth graders in the school notebook"! This young man has stayed in touch and has finished college using strategies he learned as a language learner. Through our conversations I discovered that engagement and hands-on activities that involve the whole child are long remembered. He never remembered the language arts benchmark test he took or the math assessment test he failed at the beginning of his sixth-grade year. It was the projects and the whole experience of making something meaningful to himself. Those are the types of things he was tells me about and those are the things he remembered about sixth grade.

—Veda, sixth-grade teacher

While ELLs certainly need structured support and differentiated instruction to address the challenges related to English language learning, they rarely succeed solely on the basis of academic adjustment. All students, and most particularly advanced ELLs, thrive most in classrooms where they feel creatively, emotionally, and intellectually engaged. Thus, while we all want ELLs to achieve the required levels of skill and knowledge by the end of the year, we also need to recognize that this happens naturally when they can create a relationship with something that interests them. Pioneer E. Paul Torrance talked about the "importance of falling in love with something" because learning at its best possesses that quality of heightened interest and passion. When children are highly motivated, they want to learn and discover things, and they become more alive to the world around them.

The larger challenge that ELLs face, therefore, is engagement—creating a relationship with a topic or subject. Culture and language are so fundamental to the way human societies relate to ideas, society, and environments. Culture and language do not simply act as vehicles for thought and communication; they mediate thinking (Vygotsky, 1934/1962) in significant ways. When immersing themselves in another cultural and linguistic world, ELLs become *altered*; they think and feel in new ways. Through daily social and cultural experiences, they come to adopt the attitudes and values of this world. When welcomed into the classroom, they also *alter* the learning community around them by bringing the gifts of their culture and linguistic heritage.

The strategies in this chapter focus on two fundamental steps that help ELLs to connect to an area of study: (1) designing an open learning environment for Hispanic ELLs that creates many more choices

Mrs. Sikorski was frustrated. She had been teaching the religious education classes at her church for a month and seemed to be getting nowhere with the students. "They don't listen because they don't understand English," she remarked to her assistant, a second-generation, fully bilingual, Hispanic college student. The assistant responded, "That's not it at all! They were born here and they speak and understand English fluently. But in order to engage them, you need to spark their interests and connect what you're teaching to their lives and background."

—Marisa, religious education assistant and college student

for students to learn, and (2) selecting and adapting practical, base-line strategies for meeting the learning needs of advanced Hispanic ELLs that also benefit all students. They are "teacher-friendly" because they do not require workshop training or extensive planning time. They assume that readers work in classrooms with a wide spectrum of learning abilities, needs, as well as cultural, linguistic, and economic backgrounds. These strategies are intended to assist teachers who want to do more for English language learners who also are gifted.

Creating an Open Learning Environment for Hispanic ELLs

The first question we must consider is what we mean by an open learning environment for Hispanic ELLs. For one teacher, an open learning environment could be flexible seating arrangements that allow for a variety of group and independent projects, while to another it means allowing more choices in assignments, media, and materials. No teacher has the definitive "open" classroom, but we can say that certain structures and practices tend to make learning more responsive to student needs, and this includes incorporating cultural and linguistic elements for ELLs. The structural factors of an open learning environment potentially can include physical, instructional, social-emotional, and virtual dimensions. *What* teachers do to increase openness is less important than *why* they do it and *how*.

The goal of an open learning environment is to engage students—to help them relate to subjects in an authentic way. We often talk about the importance of giving students practice in the skills they need to become more independent, more self-directed learners (setting goals, choosing assignments and projects, resources, and media, and pacing themselves). This is all true, but if students are not fundamentally engaged, cannot form relationships with the material, they lack the motivation or interest in becoming self-directed. Here are some questions to consider as you think about your own classroom:

Physical Space

- What physical features of the room or school inhibit openness?
- To what extent can you change, add to, or remove furniture to expand options?
- Does the arrangement allow ease of movement and encourage self-directed learning?

- Does the environment express the culture and language of the students?
- Does it create a sense of hominess and comfort?
- Do visual displays represent the contributions of men and women from the culture?

Think about these things:

- Visual stimulation (e.g., posters in Spanish and English, artwork by students, art by Hispanic artists, murals)
- Learning centers (with Hispanic and Spanish language materials related to topics, learning styles, interests, themes)
- Display and exhibit areas (e.g., maps of Latin American countries reflecting students' family histories, crafts, portraits of Chicano pioneers in science, math, politics, art)
- Seating arrangements (flexible design will allow for whole class instruction, small group work, and quieter areas for independent work)

Materials/Media

- Do supplies and resources reach students with different "intelligences" and learning styles?
- Do they encourage students to integrate subject areas, explore connections, and expand knowledge?
- Do they enhance flexibility in the choices students can make and the opportunities teachers can create within units of study?
- What information and communication technology applications are available?
- To what extent do these technologies enable students to use their potential for higher-level and creative thinking?
- How do students evaluate and make choices about appropriate resources for a project or assignment?

Think about these things:

- Arrangement of materials (by theme, topic, field)
- Accessibility of technology: (e.g., computers, recording devices, television, DVDs, software)
- Multilingual and multicultural (e.g., websites; networking with other Hispanic schools; networking with schools in Central and South America; biographies, poetry, fiction in Spanish or featuring Hispanic culture)

Student Engagement

- What daily routines exist to draw ELLs into the environment and the subjects at hand?
- What creative or artistic catalysts help them connect to new units?
- What classroom activities promote interest and curiosity?
- To what extent do students determine the pace and rhythm of their study?
- What choices do they make about learning goals, approaches to their work, and resources?
- Are customs, holidays, crafts, and traditions integrated into lessons?

Think about these things:

- Daily prompts (e.g., quotes, jokes, puzzling questions, unusual facts)
- Music (e.g., favorite musicians, composers, instruments from around the world)
- Student shares (e.g., stories, personal passions, aha moments)
- Student questions (e.g., mysteries, puzzles, curiosity)

Student Learning Processes and Thinking Styles

- Do assignments reflect different styles of thinking and learning?
- For example, are different "intelligences" represented in the resources and materials?
- Does the physical arrangement provide for the quiet, introspective reader as well as the small group preparing a theatrical presentation?
- To what extent are creative and artistic works of a national/ethnic background included?

Think about these things:

- Gardner's intelligences (i.e., linguistic, musical, logical-mathematical, visual-spatial, bodily-kinesthetic, interpersonal, intrapersonal, naturalist)
- Cognitive thinking styles (e.g., convergent/divergent, linear/nonlinear, inductive/deductive, rational and practical/imaginative)

- Cultural background (including values, worldviews, talents and abilities encouraged; cultural practices that develop particular ways of thinking)

Emotional/Social

- How would you characterize the atmosphere of the classroom?
- Is it visually appealing, with color, design, freedom, and artistry?
- To what extent do students choose the peers they work with?
- Are there working rules that promote civility, kindness, and sensitivity to others' needs?
- To what extent is creativity encouraged and enhanced in the classroom?

Think about these things:

- Expectations (e.g., procedures explained or criteria written down)
- Engaging catalysts for new lessons (e.g., real-world connections and creative activities)
- Encouragement and respect (risk taking is celebrated; criticism discouraged)
- Positive peer relationships (kids grouped by interests and strengths; bullying outlawed)
- Parental input (e.g., parent assistance or parent mentoring of advanced students)
- Cultural/linguistic backgrounds (i.e., sensitivity to other cultures and languages is encouraged without drawing attention to individual children)

Beginning with the classroom makes sense because a prepared space enables you to create adjustments more simply. This is particularly true if teachers include visual displays, supplies, and other resources from cultural institutes (e.g., the National Museum of Mexican Art in Chicago), as well as fliers and themes from neighborhood organizations. Students can participate in this process by sharing their stories, talents, and interests throughout the year. Educator-anthropologist Luis Moll (1992) showed the value of this when he coined the term *funds of knowledge*, a term that has helped teachers focus on the hidden strengths (knowledge, skills, abilities) of bilingual communities as guides for their education. He conducted an extensive ethnographic study of the Mexican American communities in the barrio schools of Tucson (North Central Regional Educational Laboratory, 1994). What he found was a great deal of expertise on such subjects as agriculture, economics, mining, and science. Some shared their knowledge on cultivating plants and animals and ranch management. Others knew mechanics, carpentry, masonry, and electrical wiring. Many had entrepreneurial skills and knew specific information about archeology, biology, and mathematics.

Relating this to the classroom, we can see that the more ELLs and all students can bring to the environment where they learn, the more connected they will feel. The color, design, music, stories, poems, inventions, photographs and so forth—the funds of knowledge shared from the lives of students and the teacher—foster a lively sense of community and collaborative learning. The power of bringing their lives into the classroom in this way is that it creates a bridge to the curriculum. As Moll argued, bilingual children need to be able to use the strengths that have come to them within their first language community to overcome the limitations they experience in their second-language community.

Working with parents and community members will assist teachers greatly as they will have a much clearer sense of where their students have come from and what resources, processes, and catalysts for learning will support their abilities. As Chapters 3 and 5 demonstrate, connecting with parents and cultural organizations opens doors in unexpected ways. Holidays, cultural traditions, folk arts, and community events can enliven a social studies unit, a writing assignment, or a class on measurement and design. Look for opportunities to meet parents, to attend cultural events, and to network with community groups that address local issues. In Chicago, the National Museum of Mexican Art, located in a predominantly Hispanic area, draws people from throughout the city and across the nation to view its art exhibits, attend events, take classes, and so forth. Olvera Street in Los Angeles offers similar resources and activities for students and teachers.

Schools also can consult with local Hispanic performance and art groups to enhance creative learning. Spoken word poets of all backgrounds have risen up to claim their space in this genre and some are committed to sharing with young people who struggle in ways they did. Spoken word artist Paul Flores grew up on the Tijuana-San Diego border. The founding artistic director of Chicano Messengers of Spoken Word, he has focused his work on issues of immigration and Latino identity, and he has performed widely, including an appearance on HBO's *Def Poetry Jam* with his solo show *You're Gonna Cry*.

> ## An Engaging Classroom
>
> What can you do to your classroom to engage advanced learners?
>
> How can you help all ELLs feel accepted in the learning community?
>
> How can your environment empower your advanced ELLs to use their talents?
>
> In what ways can you bring more of your students' lives to the classroom (e.g., artwork, inventions, poems, raps, crafts, cultural traditions, photographs of great moments, humorous stories)?
> Consider these questions:
>
> - Do the materials reflect the interests and learning styles of the students?
> - Are they consistent with the students' advanced developmental level, experience, and knowledge?
> - Do they prompt questions, inquiry, and a sense of wonder?
> - Do the materials stimulate higher-level thinking in different subjects?
> - Do they inspire divergent thinking and self-expression?
> - Do they enhance research skills and knowledge?
> - Do they enhance the growth of creativity?
> - Do they embrace the qualities valued by advanced learners—beauty, form, shape, quality of material, level of craftsmanship, ingenuity of design?

Learning depends on students being able to relate to people and environments—to friends, strangers, ideas, objects, languages, traditions, experiences. It rarely occurs in isolation or in abstract lessons divorced from real life. From their earliest years, ELLs have been learning through the vibrant world around them. They learn through the stories told by parents or relatives; the music, crafts, and traditions that celebrate their people; and the nooks and crannies of their neighborhood, where they play games with other children. They learn through the skills or trades of family or neighbors who share their knowledge, whether this be community organizing, electrical engineering, law, ecology, mathematics, carpentry, botany, music, or visual art. As with all children, this active process continues throughout life. Learning is *relational,* and when dealing with ELLs, this fact becomes the most important to consider.

The kind of learning that most serves advanced ELLs, and in fact all students, is one that helps them create relationships with the topics they study. A classroom that allows them more choices in how they

While few artists remember the precise moment when they decided to make art their career, David Diaz [children's book illustrator] is an exception. He clearly recalls the day in first grade when he completed a vowel worksheet that was filled with pictures of objects with incomplete words written below. A line drawing of a nose was accompanied by "n_se," and young Diaz compliantly added the "o" to the word. After that, he was inspired to use his thick red pencil to complete the picture of the face on the worksheet, and he has been drawing faces ever since. Because he did not know the term "illustrator," in a moment that he calls a mini-epiphany, Diaz realized he would become a "drawer." . . . A supportive high school teacher pointed the way for students to become artists by guiding them to competitions.

Source: From National Center for Children's Illustrated Literature (2008).

learn increases the possibility of this happening. Students connect to a topic on a deeper level, exploring different media and gathering information from teachers, librarians, parents, neighbors, and Internet sources. While we cannot make every subject enthralling to our students, we can bring into our learning environments all the elements that lead to creative engagement. These include a variety of resources centered around real-world applications, displays or exhibits of student work focused on these applications, and creative catalysts for introducing new units that allow students to approach content through their own interests and learning styles.

General Strategies for Meeting the Learning Needs of Hispanic ELLs

A key challenge in teaching ELLs is understanding their level of fluency. Contrary to what we might assume, students who express themselves easily in conversation do not necessarily possess the same facility in academic contexts (Cummins, 1981). Becoming fluent in the school halls, playground, or stores does not mean that they have mastered the kind of language proficiency needed for intellectual engagement in academic subjects. Teachers must understand that children develop social language in meaningful contexts of daily life while academic learning and its "languages" occur in more abstract forms, often with less context or immediate relevance to their experiences.

In addition, how well ELLs acquire cognitive academic language skills in English depends overwhelmingly on the level of schooling they have received in their first language (Thomas & Collier, 1997). With academic skills in their first language, 8- to 11-year-olds can reach grade level (and more if they are gifted) within five to seven years. Without this background, they may require up to ten years. The gap between social language that many gain in two years and cognitive language skills creates serious errors of judgment and assessment. Tests and observations may suggest that children are fully English proficient when they are not. Consequently, their struggle to understand and express academic concepts make them appear learning disabled.

If you are a regular classroom teacher who has had ELLs mainstreamed into your room, you can avoid a lot of frustration by knowing where these students actually are in their language development and advocate for more support services if they are needed. Also, understanding that academic literacy in the primary language enables students to excel in English provides a rationale for encouraging further education in Spanish, whether in the home, school, or community. Knowing these points enables you to provide a bridge from students' cultural, linguistic, and academic backgrounds to the concepts and skills in a unit. Helping students to make meaningful connections to new content greatly enhances both social language and cognitive academic proficiency (Echevarria, Vogt, & Short, 2004; Haynes & Zacarian, 2010).

English language learners at all levels of proficiency require instruction that builds language development into the curriculum. Some will need more accommodation than others. Essentially, though, teachers in regular classrooms can reach most ELLs by adjusting strategies they are already using. For example, they can allow students more options in how they demonstrate their understanding of a concept or in the sources and materials they use. Preparing a small group of ELLs (at a similar level of proficiency) for a lesson by introducing new topics and vocabulary through visual and oral means is another example.

It is important to point out that models for teaching ELLs often present principles that work well for *all* students. If we look at the Sheltered Instruction Observation Protocol (SIOP), for example, we can see that, aside from specific accommodations for language needs, many of the principles are those reflected in other approaches—differentiated instruction, integration of multiple intelligences and modalities for learning, and applications of the arts and creativity (which has a proven success record for bilingual students). Besides an environment that offers choices in how children process new learning, it also tends to accommodating pace and level, and offers enrichment. All these strategies help the general population as well. In addition, practices that allow flexible grouping (by interest and ability as well as language proficiency), that focus on student strengths (not just deficiencies), and that integrate students' cultures, languages, and life experiences are also goals of many districts, whether or not they achieve them.

Where SIOP differs is in its special attention to language development needs. ELLs have a program of study with language goals (listening, speaking, reading, writing) embedded in daily lessons. They make linguistic and cultural connections to the content and explore relevant vocabulary that they will encounter in a unit (terminology, subject-specific words and phrases). They use different media for understanding and communicating their ideas and understanding (e.g., cartoons, charts, designs, simulations, mime).

The following pages describe twelve strategies teachers can use in different settings that will assist Hispanic English language learners, including advanced students. We call them a "toolbox" because, while all are good principles to follow, not all apply to every situation. Feel free to pull them out and adapt them as you see fit.

A Toolbox of Strategies

1. Display Learning Goals and Tasks

All students benefit from this as it immediately increases the comfort level to know the goals and activities for the day. Keep the language simple and direct. Use images if need be. Pose questions for them to mull over. Consider posters that focus on major concepts. Images of ocean tides, for example, could accompany a question about the gravitational pull of the sun and moon. The day's goals and activities are thereby anchored by this image and question.

2. Prepare ELLs

ELLs confront vocabulary and terminology related to specific subjects and often struggle while trying to understand basic concepts and follow instructions. It would be much like engaging in a geology lesson not knowing the precise words for the instruments used in the study of rocks or the vocabulary associated with assigned tasks (Marzano & Pickering, 2005). Before introducing a unit, review the process with an eye for potential linguistic barriers. Consider different ways to share vocabulary, with words, diagrams, pictures, brief demonstrations, mime. Think about the backgrounds of your students—what sorts of professions and experiences in their families might provide a bridge to concepts in a new lesson. For example, many children participate in cooking and preparing family meals. They know how precise they have to be when adding spices, and they understand the importance of timing so that the different dishes (or parts of a dish) come together more or less at the same time. Using this as a way into a study of chemical interactions or into any study of how different elements act on, react to, or interact with each other would be helpful. As with all students, drawing on their life experience enables them to connect to their studies, but for ELLs, this is critical.

3. Allow Choices

As much as possible, provide more than one choice for ELLs or advanced students to process new concepts and to demonstrate what they know and understand. Especially allow options that assist those who may speak fluently but who need more support in the cognitive area of proficiency. This does not mean allowing students to avoid, for example, practice in writing. It means giving them a bridge into composition through other media, such as photography, videography, audio recordings, constructing or modeling with different materials, cartoons, theater, and so forth. Many ELLs who find the blank page paralyzing can make the leap by responding to and exploring ideas through more accessible means. Along with the language support, advanced ELLs may need assignments that challenge them more.

Here are some changes to consider.

- From a single source or process to multiple sources or processes. Students write a report on an important event in the life of a family member *after* recording, sketching, miming, designing, or blogging a chronology of the event first.
- From learning about words (through looking them up) to exploring the linguistic sources of words—their history, linguistic origins, changes through time, and current use—and creating biographies of or multimedia compositions about these words.
- From mainstream American culture to multicultural. They use Hispanic source material (e.g., biographies, reports, and stories in Spanish and English; art and photography; video; podcasts; traditional celebrations and customs; games; objects) to re-create historical events or to examine the scientific principles employed by Mexican engineers and scientists (e.g., Guillermo Gonzalez Camarena's invention of the "chromoscopic adapter for television equipment," an early color television transmission system).
- From whole class instruction to small group learning opportunities based on language level. Students receive some downtime from English-only instruction to engage with each other in

Spanish. They support each other during assigned tasks. And they receive assistance from the teacher or volunteer assistant to clarify instructions or to support comprehension or writing skills.

- From predominantly academic to an integrated creative-academic approach. Students create brief ensemble theatrical pieces based by the short poems and stories of Eduardo Galeano's (1993) *Walking Words* (based on urban and rural folklore of Latin America). With the teacher's support, they explore different narrative styles and use their bodies, props, or costumes to express their understanding and interpretation.

4. Encourage Goal Setting

Support ELLs in setting alternative learning goals for themselves. This begins with the previous suggestion to display the day's (or week's) schedule in the classroom. Helping students set goals has a powerful effect on their confidence and achievement. Particularly in larger projects that may extend through the course of a unit, students need practice in creating smaller steps. When students learn how to break up a project into manageable pieces, two things happen. First, they become more confident and secure in directing their abilities toward goals that feel more manageable. Second, they experience their own progress as they complete one goal after the next and this enhances their sense of efficacy as learners. Fear of falling short due to language difficulties becomes more problematic for students who lack experience in goal setting. Instead of "I must write a final report in a language I'm still learning," students focus on a more realistic goal: "I can first fill out the KWL chart—what I already *know*, what I *want* to know, and what I've *learned* so far. Then, I can talk to my teacher on a source list for the research I need to do," and so on. (See Del Siegle's Web page on goal setting at www.gifted .uconn.edu/siegle/SelfEfficacy/section8.html.)

5. Determine Prior Knowledge

While ELLs may take five to seven years to master cognitive academic language (Haynes & Zacarian, 2010), some may appear prematurely at your door and still need accommodations in written composition, vocabulary, and comprehension in some subjects. One of the most important questions to consider is: How do I best determine what these students know given their language needs? A common error is to assume that language deficits extend to intellectual ability. It is important, therefore, to find ways to discover what ELLs understand in a geometric calculation, the ecology of water, or the music and rhythm of poetic verse. Conferring with parents, bilingual interpreters, or community members who know the children can sometimes be eye-opening. ELLs enter our rooms with abilities, experiences, and skills, much of which they either hide or lay aside, assuming they have no value in an English-speaking world. Give them credit for the knowledge and skill they possess and help them create alternative assignments that support their comprehension and composition in English. Avoid too many drill-and-practice assignments that make them feel trapped in remedial exercises. Here are some useful ways to assess prior knowledge and skill.

- Daily observation
- KWL chart
- Consultation with other teachers and parents
- Portfolio of prior work (from home or school)
- Informal discussion with students

6. Accommodate Pace

In any population, there are always students who know more at the beginning of a lesson and need a faster pace to stay engaged. Most teachers accommodate different levels as much as they can, either through providing different tiers within an assignment, allowing students to skip content they already know and move on to more challenging assignments, or variations of these. With ELLs, acceleration becomes a little more difficult as teachers need to assess level of mastery in the context of a developing fluency in English and to incorporate language needs in more advanced assignments. For native speakers, acceleration may involve assigning more difficult texts to read that would not work for ELLs. However, providing alternative media and activities (e.g., diagrams, visual images, instructions in Spanish, group learning with other ELLs) would serve them well. Creative thinking, as shown in number seven, also frees advanced ELLs to extend their mental powers in new directions. Accelerated and creative thinking often coexist in such students. Presenting an open-ended math problem, for example, allows them to discover their own formulas through using their hands, testing ideas, working with peers, and formulating hypotheses.

7. Accommodate Creative Needs

Creativity serves not only ELLs but all students. Far more than the enrichment often associated with it, creative teaching provides dynamic alternatives to traditional study, fosters original thought, and inspires students to become more engaged learners. Adopting a creative mind-set to everything you do in the classroom will help you to exploit the full potential of creativity and the arts, regardless of any specific skills or expertise you possess (see Chapter 8). As many teachers have proven, creativity is not about paintbrushes and poems; it is a way of thinking and being. Consider how the following general principles might apply to your ELLs.

- Present open-ended assignments that ask students to draw on their creative and imaginative responses, their life experiences, cultures, and artistic inclinations.
- Create a safe environment for out-of-the-box learning and honor any and all creative ideas.
- Celebrate boldness or risk taking, however great or small.
- Model and teach coping skills to deal with feelings of frustration, being overwhelmed, and self-doubt.
- Support students' trust in their own creative powers through open questioning. Point out the hidden jewels in their work and guide them to new resources and materials.
- Provide opportunities to correct errors, refine visions, improve, elaborate, and emphasize creativity as an ongoing process rather than a means to an end product.
- Make arts activities and resources accessible to ELLs (e.g., visual art materials, mime, theater games, design, art designs from found objects).
- Explore a variety of venues for students to show, demonstrate, perform, or exhibit what they know or have learned.

8. Accommodate Interests

Provide advanced ELLs opportunities to explore their interests. Again, the KWL chart or something similar will enable students to become curious and invest more of themselves in their studies. Former U.S. Secretary of Education, Terrell Bell, said: "There are three important things to remember about education. The first one is motivation, the second is motivation, and the third is motivation" (Ames, 1990). In a similar vein, E. Paul Torrance provided guidance in a piece that has become the inspiration for many students, young and old. "The Importance of Falling in Love With Something" (Torrance, 1983) exhorts young people to pursue what most calls to them and to honor their greatest strengths. Knowing that engagement propels learning for ELLs (and all ELLs), try to incorporate their interests wherever you can. Their challenges will become less burdensome; their self-doubts will give way to the excitement they feel. Consider these possibilities:

- Use student interest inventories, open-ended opportunities to share new interests or curiosities, or student-generated questions ("What I've always wanted to know is . . .") to help students discover what they want to learn.
- Structure units that have some flexibility for you to incorporate student interests in ways that also support their language needs.
- Communicate with families and others who know the students (e.g., teachers or leaders in art workshops, youth programs, or community events they have attended).
- Have all students design their own portfolio—folder or container—where they can collect work from either home or class that they particularly value.
- Create opportunities for students to exhibit or share student interests (e.g., artwork, performances, inventions, collections, experiments, writing).

9. Promote Peer Relationships

As mentioned earlier, learning occurs best when ELLs have frequent opportunities to participate and interact with each other (Echevarria et al., 2004). For example, paired and group work with students who have a similar linguistic and cultural background allows them to explore new content-specific vocabulary or learn in a safe and comfortable social group (Haynes & Zacarian, 2010). At the same time, more advanced ELLs also may want to pair off with English-speakers who share their interests and abilities. In general, ELLs who demonstrate noticeable gains in academic language proficiency need to participate in small groups that include native speakers. Social and emotional difficulties often diminish when these students realize that their talents and experiences have as much value as those of English-speakers. Here are some examples:

- Pair more advanced ELLs together to work on an alternative assignment (e.g., a challenging science experiment or a design for a class research and mural project depicting immigration in their school).
- Create an interest-based group of Spanish- and English-speakers, in cases where ELLs have a higher level of proficiency, in order to increase confidence in their developing abilities.

- Collaborate with another teacher to combine advanced ELLs in a cluster group; share responsibilities for the group.
- For ELLs of any level who demonstrate high motivation and interest, try to establish a mentoring relationship with a parent or community member who possesses particular talents or expertise in an area of interest.

10. Find Local Talent to Open Students' Minds

Nothing excites students more than exposure to worlds they have never known before. An artist, writer, or entrepreneur who shares skills or expertise (related to a unit or lesson) can be a turning point for students. Spoken word artists have ignited young minds across the country, enabling them to connect to issues around identity, history, society, and language. Business people have taught about the market economy as students learn about entrepreneurship and create their own ideas for a service or product. Given that many Spanish-speaking communities struggle in economically depressed neighborhoods, strong leaders in the arts, humanities, business, and civic projects provide a vision of new possibilities.

An African American artist in Detroit offers a striking example of this. Painter and sculptor Tyree Guyton looked for ways to turn Detroit's urban blight back on itself through a range of colorful and exuberant art works in the struggling neighborhood where he lived. Made from found objects and including everything from painted shoes to elaborate installations, Guyton's projects gradually transformed the city streets into an art gallery. Young people encountered a world they never knew existed—one that made them think and gave them a sense of worth and a feeling of beauty as a people. Giving ELLs exposure to people like Guyton reveals worlds never imagined before and can sometimes benefit these students more than years of schooling.

11. Provide for Independent Learning

In small groups, pairs, or on their own, ELLs who feel more comfortable in the classroom should have opportunities to do more independent projects. A student may want to do a journalistic investigation into Mexican entrepreneurship in the United States—an ambitious goal that could quickly become unmanageable. Instead, guide this student (or pair or group of students) to interview local shopkeepers about how they started their businesses and survived the ups and downs of beginning a new life in the neighborhood. With independent projects, you have to consider the level of planning and supervision involved (Can you manage it? Can you find helpers who can assist?), the level of ability and skill required for the ELLs to work more independently, and identified language needs and support for the students to complete the project (Are there assistants? Are there different media for them to use in addition to reading and writing? What sort of preparation and support will they need?). Here are some independent learning skills for you to consider as you think about this option for the ELLs in your class.

- Performing academic tasks without adult intervention for longer periods
- Understanding at least the main points of an assignment
- Locating—either on their own or in paired or group situations—different, yet reliable sources of information
- Demonstrating some level of initiative, as well as persistence, in a challenging task
- Applying basic organization skills to meet deadlines, such as identify manageable steps, creating a time line, clarifying responsibilities
- Identifying areas where they will need help (e.g., language support, skills, direction)
- Achieving some self-awareness as learners (knowing their strengths and weaknesses) and focusing on personal strengths and aptitudes

12. Encourage Self-Assessment

To some, self-assessment may seem unrealistic or impractical for ELLs. But what we are talking about here are strategies to help ELLs recognize their own progress and what they have learned. Nothing could be more important for those who perpetually feel a need to "catch up" with their peers. Even gifted Spanish-speakers can lag behind in some areas and judge themselves harshly in consequence. The KWL chart can assist here, but any means for making growth visual to ELLs will work. They could create their own record: What did they take away from a lesson or unit that they did not know or have before? How confident do they feel with a new task that they did not feel before? How many new words do they know? How does their writing compare with what they did last month? It is so easy for all of us to become blind to our growth in the face of new challenges. For ELLs this becomes a greater obstacle because the need for greater proficiency feels like an unending challenge. Three examples follow:

Anecdotal records: For ELLs, this can take the form of audio or video recordings, informal interviews, written responses in a journal, or a display that relates to their learning experiences. Example: In a small group project, students focus on four key questions (displayed by the teacher):

1. What do I feel I am doing well in this project?

2. What is hard for me? What do I think my difficulty is (Do I not understand something? Is it a skill I still need support in?)?

3. What do I like the most about this assignment?

4. What do I enjoy least?

Criteria lists: Displaying, in simple English (with visuals if necessary), a list of criteria for an assigned task helps ELLs visualize the sequence of action steps in a project, monitor their progress, and not lose focus or devote too much time to one item. A criteria list for a project on a science project could include the following:

1. My project draws on at least two sources and one Web site and focuses on one question: How does an environment I know relate to the survival of a specific animal? (A place where there is a lot of milkweed and the monarch butterfly.) What feature of this animal makes it able to survive in this environment? (The colors of a monarch butterfly signal to local birds that they are toxic as food.)

2. My creative display (combining text, scientific sketches, collage, and so on) tells how an animal finds its basic needs for food, shelter, and protection in a specific kind of environment.

3. My final project shows the relationship between a species and its environment and includes a map, a sketch of one feature of an animal that helps it to survive (long, pointed wings of a swallow that allow maneuverability for hunting insects), and what kind of environment it needs that provides an abundance of insects.

Follow-up: It is helpful for ELLs to reflect on what they have learned and what skill they feel more able to apply. Questions can help them see their own process and identify what they do well, how they have grown, and where they may need more practice.

1. What did I learn that I did not know before?

2. What about the final product (display, report, performance) do I feel good about?

3. What parts of the assignment were the hardest for me? Why?

4. What things might I change about the final product to make it better? What would I need in order to do this (more practice at a skill, clarification on instructions, more creative ways to express what I learned)?

Applications to the Classroom

Applying these general strategies enables you to work them into your daily teaching when ELLs can most benefit from them and when you have the time and resources to do so. Treat these twelve strategies as a toolbox you can adjust to the unique situation you face in your district, school, and student population. You will not use all the tools all the time. The needs of ELLs, like all students, shift frequently, depending on what you are teaching and what strengths and needs they bring to the subject. A quick learner may not always do well in an accelerated unit, particularly if it involves the subtleties of language and written composition. An ELL with artistic or creative talent still needs to acquire an understanding of grammar and to practice reading skills that will help her become a stronger writer. A child with a sophisticated understanding of certain math principles may benefit more from the creative application of this knowledge than from simply learning new topics.

Teachers in regular classrooms rarely have the time and resources to go all out for ELLs or any other special population. Yet, with the No Child Left Behind Act of 2001 (NCLB) in full force, districts today have to test students' academic language ability, whereas in prior years, they only had to assess basic speaking, reading, and writing. For ELLs who are gifted as well, building language goals into assigned work is even more urgent as

> **What Actions Can You Take?**
>
> - Create alternatives for ELLs to fulfill an assignment
> - Prepare ELLs who need it with a preview of upcoming lessons (concepts, vocabulary, and so on)
> - Adjust the pace for advanced ELLs who need more challenge but also require some language support
> - Integrate creative or artistic modalities for learning new concepts
> - Incorporate student interests, cultures, and life experiences
> - Group ELLs together or, when appropriate, pair them with native speakers who have similar interests or abilities

their abilities can, in many instances, exceed their English proficiency. So teachers face a dilemma: What are reasonable expectations given the limits on my time, resources, and expertise? As with all your other students, you will need to make choices based on three overriding concerns.

Ask yourself the following three questions.

1. What needs of my ELLs (including advanced students) are most pressing right now?

Examples
- Better reading comprehension in language arts assignments
- Clearer understanding of terminology in science class
- More support for students whose writing skills lag significantly behind superior verbal fluency
- More support for creative and artistic gifts and interests

2. In which areas of the curriculum do they struggle most with respect to their level of proficiency in English?

Examples
- Language arts—primarily written composition
- Verbal expression of ideas that involve higher-level thinking (due to undeveloped cognitive language skills)
- Difficulties understanding teacher's verbal questions during a math assignment that involves inductive reasoning
- Problems responding to and interpreting materials and references to popular culture

3. What strategies would specifically target these high priority areas for my bilingual students, including the high achieving ones?

Examples
- Using creative catalysts, accessible to ELLs, that draw on their strengths, spur their thinking, and introduce them to the main concepts in a lesson
- Providing vocabulary support and bilingual books (including "real" literary works—poems, stories, biographies) that enable students to check their comprehension
- Clarifying steps of an assignment with visuals
- Pairing ELLs with native speakers at their level of academic ability (especially good for gifted ELLs)
- Creating small groups of ELLs to nurture a Spanish-speaking community who can collaborate on some assignments

Not all of these examples apply to your classroom. But keeping these three questions firmly in mind will help you streamline your preparation. In many cases, you can assist ELLs by building these strategies into the unit you have planned for the whole class. This works well if you begin in areas where expanding what you are already doing is most manageable. Where is it easiest for you to allow a more creative process in preparation for an environmental science unit? How can ELLs (and all students) have more freedom in selecting materials that support their understanding? In what ways can you use bilingual essays to bolster understanding of English usage and composition? As you become more confident and skilled in supporting these students on a smaller scale, you can increase your repertoire of strategies.

For advanced ELLs, you may need to make further adjustments as the discrepancies between ability and performance can, in some cases, be even more exaggerated. ELLs who learn quickly do not always show their struggles because they appear to function at the level of native speakers. "They're doing well!" you may say. The problem here is that their ability actually exceeds this level, but their cognitive language proficiency has not caught up with it. A child who loves science, for example, may want to explore solar technology but struggles with the materials she has found on the subject. The language is too technical and the visuals, without the explanations, make no sense. In this case, the needs are the same as other ELLs but at a different level. Teachers can still assist by any of the following actions.

- Clarifying technical terminology and concepts
- Gesturing (with props!) each step in a process
- Pairing the student with another native speaking student with similar abilities and interests
- Finding written sources in Spanish (For gifted students, Spanish language sources are critical in situations where students feel held back by the language barrier.)

A Review of What You Can Do

In this chapter, we have explored a number of strategies that support the emotional, social, and academic needs of English language learners (including the gifted). Some, such as creating a rich and engaging learning environment or adjusting the pace and level of instruction, you may already be doing. Others, like giving ELLs more choices in setting goals or developing the skills of self-assessment, you may not.

Some strategies appear more manageable than others. Wherever you stand on this spectrum, the demand remains to respond in some way to the most urgent problems of Hispanic ELLs, including the gifted. Academic standards for ELLs exist, whether or not these students attend schools with language support services. Classroom teachers who want to help these students realize their potential often ask what they can do—right now, right here—to make this achievement possible.

To review, the environment is the foundation for any intervention that actually benefits ELLs. It offers the nurturance, inspiration, openness, safety, and sense of community that calm the troubled hearts of students who feel foreign and isolated. The rich resources they find there remind them of the world of their home, their parents, and their relatives far away, but they also entice them to explore the English-speaking world they know less.

The toolbox of strategies begins with this stimulating, supportive environment in place. These strategies—familiar to most teachers—work well for ELLs (including the gifted) as long as they are adapted to accommodate students' special language needs. For those who have so little time at their disposal, this would mean starting with what they do effectively and building from there. Few teachers can devote time and resources to design alternative learning experiences that require extensive follow-up and supervision. What they can do, however, is build on the teaching practices that already work well and expand on these by experimenting with the strategies proposed in this chapter. To serve the needs of both ELLs (including the gifted) and English-speaking students, this can sometimes be a juggling act. But the process enables teachers to become more adaptable and flexible in responding to these needs as they shift and change over time. In the end, teachers will expand their repertoire of strategies and will be better equipped to serve the growing population of English language learners in their district.

8

Program Options for Advanced Hispanic ELLs

Putting Your Strategies to Work

There is no shortage of research and teaching models for addressing the needs of English language learners, and certainly no agreement across the country as to the best approach for teaching them. These students present a wide range of learning needs in the first place. Like any other population, they also include the same variation of ability, knowledge, and skill. So, when approaching Hispanic ELLs who also present signs of giftedness, teachers face a double dilemma: how to support language development while also responding to exceptional ability.

Designing programs for advanced Hispanic ELLs with varying levels of proficiency works best if teachers keep three key points distinctly in mind:

1. *Students need to be inspired, not just motivated.* Inspiration is less talked about in education than motivation and engagement, but the fact is that without inspiration, students cannot become motivated or engaged for long. To inspire is to "breathe life into." Inspiration is oxygen for talented ELLs who need to feel that they belong and can

thrive in the school environment. Inspiring them means giving them something worth exploring. It sometimes means abandoning textbooks for real literature, connecting to their interests and cultures, or finding a more creative catalyst for a new unit.

2. *Students need to see and experience their greatest assets.* ELLs, however gifted, feel behind. Begin with what they *have*—their funds of knowledge, as Moll (1992) called it, their talents, abilities, experiences, and cultural worlds. Equally important, help them to see and acknowledge their assets. When they experience what they do well, they will have the confidence to tackle their problems. This is not only true of ELLs, but all human beings. We can all tackle difficult tasks if we know we are bringing something to the table.

3. *Students need to address their special needs from a position of strength.* This will become much easier if the first two are in place. We can address deficiencies more effectively from the foundation of inspiration and ability. ELLs who struggle to achieve more proficiency in academic contexts get into a "zone" when they are fully engaged in something they love. They naturally draw on their inner strengths to address weaker areas. They still have to perform the sometimes arduous task of honing their language skills, but this process becomes less burdensome or intimidating when the foundation is in place.

These three key points are not steps in a sequence, but integrated into a whole. Programming for advanced ELLs (and in fact all students) only works well when these pieces are in place. Without inspiration, ELLs feel little motivation or engagement. Without a connection to their strengths and heritage, ELLs struggle to develop a higher level of proficiency. Programs, models, and all the resources imaginable cannot accomplish what these three simple points can do.

Identification of Strengths and Needs

Programs of any kind begin with knowing the students. Unfortunately, this often translates into assessing ability on the basis of standardized testing or on superficial evaluations that do not accommodate students' cultural and linguistic differences or their hidden strengths and talents. One of the inescapable realities of public schools is standardized testing that significantly limits teachers' own creative responses to the needs of ELLs, particularly advanced ones.

Spanning the past 40 years, the new testing movement has tried to remedy biases related to such factors as language differences, ethnocentric test items, inappropriate norm sampling, and issues of test administration (e.g., time limits, lack of motivation, test anxiety). For Hispanic students, instruments have included a shortened version of the Wechsler Intelligence Scale for Children-Revised (WISC-R) in both English and Spanish, the Abbreviated Binet for the Disadvantaged (ABDA), Raven Progressive Matrices test, the Torrance Tests of Creative Thinking (TTCT), and the Naglieri Nonverbal Ability Test (NNAT). These tests accommodate the linguistic and cultural differences of ELLs, but are far from comprehensive.

The only way to make assessment less biased is to stop conferring more importance on tests than on other sources of information. Observations, informal interviews, student projects, and creative compositions have equal validity. This is not a new idea. In the 1980s, the Encendiendo Uno Llama programs (Barstow, 1987) identified gifted bilingual students by examining student work. Pioneers such as Torrance (1977), Bruch (1975), and Bernal (1981) concluded from their research that assessing ability in students from other cultures can only be fair if schools consult the definitions of talent and ability *within those cultures.* Baldwin (2003) presented the following points as a guide for identifying the gifted among low socioeconomic and culturally different communities (pp. 85–86).

- Giftedness can be expressed through a variety of behaviors.
- Giftedness expressed in one area (as just listed) is just as important as giftedness expressed in another.
- Giftedness in any area can be a clue to the presence of potential giftedness in another area, or a catalyst for the development of giftedness in another area.
- A total ability profile is crucial in planning an educational program for gifted children.
- All populations have gifted children who exhibit behaviors that are indicative of giftedness.

The following chart will help you visualize ways you can plan instruction for your ELLs, including the more advanced ones. The

KNWL Chart for Advanced Hispanic ELLs

What students *know*:

Level of mastery in topics involving more or less English

Pace of learning in different subjects

Cultural strengths and traditions

Related experiences and skills

What students *need*:

Culture-sensitive environment

Differentiated instruction for ELLs

Creative sources and materials (multiple intelligences)

Language support

What students *want* to learn:

Interest-based topics and activities

Ideas and skills that engage preferred learning styles

Subjects related to special talents and skills

Fields that apply to prior experiences

What students have *learned:*

More challenging concepts and skills

New discoveries due to open-ended assignments

Areas of ability and strength

Strategies that address language needs

main question to consider is: If we begin with their interests, talents, and learning styles, how can we most inspire them as learners and use the strengths within them to address their special needs?

One option is to modify the KWL chart to accommodate the needs of English language learners. As an example, here is the KNWL chart: K (what they *know*), N (what they *need* to support language development and accommodate cultural differences), W (what they *want* to learn), and L (what they have *learned*).

By identifying strengths and needs, this kind of chart can guide programming choices, whether these are class assignments, mentorships, independent studies, or after-school workshops. It focuses on priorities, the specific activities that help ELLs realize their potential and what they have learned and gained from one experience to the next.

The following pages explore the different paths you can take to meet the needs of advanced (and all) Hispanic ELLs.

School-Based Program Options for Advanced Spanish-Speakers

Students from other cultures and linguistic backgrounds can benefit from teaching practices that you use or at least understand. They require different adjustments, but you can structure them to accommodate advanced ability as well as linguistic strengths and weaknesses.

Differentiating for Advanced Hispanic ELLs

Differentiated instruction has given the general education field more flexibility in responding to the special needs of diverse learners. When it comes to Hispanic or any other population of ELLs, teachers naturally adjust instruction to address whatever language needs present themselves. Those who arrive at their school with exceptional talents most likely will find their abilities unnoticed, if not unseen. This is particularly damaging for students of lower income, whose families may not realize what such potential can do for their children's future.

One of the most useful concepts in differentiation is the three-pronged focus on *content, process,* and *products* (Tomlinson, 1999). Keeping these three areas in mind, we can effectively build on the academic and creative strengths of Hispanic ELLs, while also bolstering their language skills. Such an approach would ensure that an insightful, analytical thinker could research a topic of interest and display her or his findings in a multimedia format, rather than postpone this opportunity because of language-related difficulties. Also, honing writing or reading skills becomes less arduous when students can use their potential to do something they love.

Figure 8.1   Questions for Planning Instruction for ELLs

Content	Process	Products
• Does the unit or lesson allow advanced ELLs to learn at a pace and level appropriate for them? • Does it provide for cultural and language differences through multilingual sources, an emphasis on multiple intelligences, and different modalities? • Does it relate to their interests, talents, cultural strengths and values, and experiences?	• Does the unit or lesson allow for different learning styles or include nontraditional "intelligences"? • Does it provide for the different grouping needs of advanced ELLs, who sometimes need to work with other ELLs and other times to collaborate with a mixed group of gifted students? • Do they incline toward more creative thinking and intuiting, or do they enjoy the process of discovery through induction and logic?	• Does the assignment give them other ways to show what they have learned in addition to speaking and writing? And can they take it to a higher level without being held back by language? • Can they apply special talents or skills that enable them to expand their exploration and understanding in significant ways? • Can they use a variety of technologies and modes of communication (including the arts) to strengthen their English language skills?

Figure 8.1 offers some questions for you to explore as you plan instruction for your ELLs.

We can only imagine the frustration of gifted ELLs. They acquire English more quickly than their peers, but, depending on their background and prior education, they may struggle at the academic proficiency level. This means that while they crave a real intellectual challenge, they feel constrained by their less developed proficiency in English. On top of that, the adults in their lives think they are doing "just fine" because they speak, comprehend, read, and write at an appropriate level for their age. Even in cases where teachers recognize special talent, they often do not know how to accommodate the needs of a gifted ELL. Adjusting the level of an assignment certainly allows advanced native speakers to use their analytical abilities and creative thinking. But for ELLs, teachers also have to consider the language/culture dimension. For example, they must ensure that sources include texts in translation and that students have a range of materials—things they can manipulate, arrange, and design; things they can observe and examine; and things they can observe, hear, and feel. They need to think about how to alter assignments so that students no longer work on strengthening language skills at the expense of intellectual and creative talent.

Think about these questions as you consider how you can adjust instruction in math, science, language arts, or social studies. What can you do for advanced Hispanic ELLs who excel on an academic level but still need some support in their developing English language proficiency?

- Can you pair them with other advanced students who may or may not be Hispanic but who share their passions and interests?
- Can you integrate Hispanic histories, traditions, celebrations, and art works to create a bridge to a subject?
- Can you challenge their academic and creative gifts by introducing sources that do not always demand a high level of English proficiency? These include science equipment, math Web sites, software programs for mapmaking, art materials, and the like.
- Can you find suitable Hispanic professionals from outside the school (e.g., business people, artists, scientists) who can inspire and challenge advanced students, particularly those from Hispanic backgrounds?
- Can you examine a class assignment and find ways to add another layer of complexity that requires such thinking strategies, such as comparing, analyzing, synthesizing, and interpreting?

The more opportunities you can create to allow students to choose interest-based resources and activities to complete assignments, the more you can reach high-ability Hispanic ELLs. By opening up a unit of study in this way, you also provide choices (e.g., more or less difficult, creative, in-depth) that benefit many more children in the classroom. This is important because a common sentiment among many educators is this: "Spending so much time on a small minority detracts me from the rest of the class; are the needs of the few more important than those of the many?" Yet, classrooms that become more flexible and open to student abilities and interests invariably benefit everyone. A disinterested child who rarely excels in academics suddenly thrives when allowed to learn in a more creative way. The number of students who underachieve due to a lack of engagement or interest is often unknown until teachers begin offering more choices.

Benjamin Bloom's taxonomy is a bit worn around the edges, according to some teachers, but the revised one (Anderson & Krathwohl, 2001) provides more direction for accommodating advanced learners. The revision replaces nouns with verbs, which makes them easier to translate into the classroom. For example, the *creating* category replaces the *synthesis* of the original, which applies to all kinds of learning experiences, whether students are exploring new solutions to a scientific riddle or interpreting a poem. Here is the revised version:

- Remembering
- Understanding
- Applying
- Analyzing
- Evaluating
- Creating

The verb forms make adjusting assignments easier. Without having to fundamentally change a unit or lesson, you can use this revision to create higher levels of thinking for advanced Hispanic students. The following are a couple of ways you can vary instruction in one class.

Scenario 1: Most of the class participates at the remembering and understanding stages of a history lesson and those who complete this advance to the applying stage. More advanced students choose related activities from one of the higher stages—analyzing, evaluating, or creating.

Example: In a lesson on the Civil Rights Act of 1964, the class learns about the specific injustices the act addressed and why this was a landmark change in U.S. history. Another group applies this act to current issues related to injustice, examining how Spanish-speaking Americans have had to struggle for their rights (e.g., Mexican American civil rights movement). Another group of students use their advanced understanding and imagination to compose poems in Spanish and English, and create a visual art display of the history they have explored.

Scenario 2: All students begin assigned work at the remembering and understanding levels. Advanced learners who finish an assignment early extend their study—with teacher assistance—to higher levels of thinking through such processes as analyzing findings, comparing ideas, and interpreting evidence.

Example: In a study of solar energy, the class learns how solar energy cells are constructed and how they absorb sunlight and convert them to solar energy power. Advanced students (including Spanish-speaking learners) apply the principles they have learned to the construction of solar ovens from cardboard boxes, aluminum foil, and black construction paper. They create designs of how solar power works and imagine ways it can power homes and everyday appliances.

In addition to adjusting for higher levels of thinking and doing, teachers also need to think about the *depth levels*. Advanced learners are inclined to explore a topic more deeply, inquiring into its roots, posing new questions, and examining related fields or sources. This sort of study requires more time, which teachers often cannot provide. However, they can design a project on a smaller scale or break it into more manageable pieces. Though it assumes different forms, an in-depth study distinguishes itself in the following ways:

- It is open-ended, ongoing, and does not end with one answer.
- It allows students to draw upon prior experience, interests, cultural knowledge, and special skills and talents.
- It enables students to participate in setting goals and determining a plan of action appropriate to their needs.
- It presents questions that inspire further inquiry.
- It allows students to explore more fields when appropriate and beneficial to the project or topic.
- It offers more choices in how students present, produce, or express their findings.

This kind of *depth* learning sounds impractical. But it can become significantly more practical when structured on a scale that teachers can manage. Consider some of the less time-consuming examples in the list that follows.

What can you do for Hispanic ELLs who want to explore a topic in more depth?

- Would recordings and photographs of neighbors and family members telling their stories enhance a student's understanding the importance of primary sources in the making of history?
- Can you extend a unit on geometry to include students' interest in applying the mathematics of shape, line, angle, and so forth to identify species of flora and fauna—and to depict these in designs?
- What resources would engage their interests and learning styles and enable them to expand their understanding of a topic or subject?
- In what ways can you help them gain the knowledge and skill they need to pursue a particular subject?

As mentioned before, the whole class will benefit from opening up your classroom to different learning paths. With new resources, assignments, and questions to explore, more students thrive in ways you might not anticipate. Depth can be more successful in engaging students' curiosity because it frees them to pursue their interests through other learning modalities, such as independent study options, creativity, and the arts.

Interest-Based Independent Learning

A student can be academically or creatively talented without necessarily having the skills to work independently on a project. But advanced ELLs (or any other students) who can follow directions with less assistance and know how to pace themselves well may be ready for more independent learning situations. Teachers with less time can begin on a smaller scale. More commonly used strategies like *anchor activities* and *choice boards* require less planning time and allow advanced students to do more advanced and often more creative work.

Anchor activities are alternative assignments, anchored to the unit or skill being taught, that give students the freedom to select their own materials and resources and proceed with their assignment without much direction or supervision from teachers. A choice board often takes the form of a chart with a wider range of activities, resources, and topics related to the subject at hand. It takes some time to plan choice boards so that students can work more or less independently, but it ultimately saves time. In both these options,

- What arrangement would work best for your advanced ELLs students?
- What choices could you include that allow advanced ELLs to build on their knowledge and skill in different modalities (e.g., creative, artistic) and intelligences (e.g., visual, kinesthetic, linguistic)?
- Would they benefit from working in pairs or alone?
- Can you provide extra time for them to complete alternative assignments?
- What anchor activities provide greater difficulty and flexibility for talented ELLs and also reduce dependency on language skills?
- What options on a choice board can draw on resources that ELLs feel comfortable with, such as science equipment, measuring devices, or art materials?

clearly written directions (accompanied by visuals if needed) enable advanced ELLs to make more choices that draw on their talents and interests. A science unit, for example, might offer an anchor activity that includes visual art, mapmaking, mineral kits, computer software, hand lenses, or recording equipment.

Independent Study

Some advanced students, including ELLs, have the ability and drive to undertake longer independent study projects. For these students, anchor activities and choice boards often do not go far enough. However, they can only choose this option if they have the maturity, skill, and experience to work independently for an extended time. Sometimes teachers assume that advanced learners can do independent studies because of their high potential, but this is not always the case. Independent studies require a certain amount of strategizing, prioritizing, self-monitoring, and focus—abilities they may not have developed yet. In addition, Hispanic ELLs also may require advanced language instruction in areas where they need greater skill (e.g., in understanding contexts, deciphering meanings, recognizing tone and irony, interpreting texts and data).

In some cases, advanced Spanish-speakers can undertake this kind of challenge if they are paired with another student. Alternatively, a family member or mentor from the community could help inspire gifted ELLs, support their progress, and assist them in meeting deadlines. As described in Chapter 6, parents of Hispanic ELLs play a vital role in partnering with teachers and maintaining communication between home and school. Teachers can manage this process through a "contract" that clarifies the learning goals, the steps to take, and the conditions for satisfaction. The main objective is to structure the independent study so that ELLs know what to do at each phase of their project and how to pace themselves in order to complete it.

The guidelines in the box offer examples of how you can assist students in the process. Feel free to adapt them to your own students' projects.

This process can be scaled up or down depending on what is best for your students and you. Bear in mind too that you do not have to structure every step in detail if the students feel enthused about the project, can monitor their own progress to some extent, and have enough built-in support for their language development needs.

> ### Independent Studies for Advanced ELLs
>
> - Help ELLs discover what most inspires and interests them and decide what specific question, topic, or dimension they want to explore.
> - Assist students in identifying their knowledge about the topic, as well as past experiences, skills, and special talents they bring to the topic.
> - Establish appropriate goals according to level of difficulty, interest, and learning style. Think about big ideas, knowledge, and skills.
> - Work with ELLs to settle on a product that combines different media, equipment, and materials for students to think more creatively and learn without the usual constraints of the classroom.
> - Clearly explain and list expectations: what they need to explore about a question or topic (content), the steps they need to take to accomplish this (process), and the results of their exploration in whatever form is most appropriate for them (products).
> - Determine support you may need to provide along the way (e.g., language assistance in reading or writing, setting priorities, pacing, and so on).
> - Make changes to the project based on student progress, organizational skill, mastery of the subject, interest, and learning styles.
> - Mentor the student when needed.

Creativity and the Arts

In education and in society, we tend to think of creativity in terms of doing something, such as painting, composing, designing, or writing. Yet, back in the 1960s and 1970s, some forward thinking educators saw creativity primarily as a way of being (e.g., Maslow, 1968; May, 1975). We can talk about a creative attitude or experience, for example, without this leading to a product of any kind. In *self-actualization* (Maslow, 1968), human beings live lives of spontaneity and freedom. Creative beings give themselves license to be original and distinguish themselves less by credentials or productions but by their keen sense of wonder (Carson, 1998).

May (1975), Maslow (1968), and Rogers (1970) found several primary characteristics of creative people.

- They become deeply immersed in the moment (experiencing a temporary suspension of time, past and present).
- They feel open to their experience as an original event (leaving the past behind and treating the present as new).

- They accept themselves as they are, free of others' judgments (validating their individuality without reservation).

Understanding creativity as a way of being (rather than a gift bestowed on an elite few) can bring a radical shift in the way we think and teach. If creativity is a way of being, accessible to all human beings in some form, than it becomes a resource we can all use without wondering if we have the credentials or "the gift." For advanced students, most particularly Ells, creativity is food and water, as it releases them from language-based sources and activities. High intellectual demand and creativity work together and enable students to make discoveries they never would in more traditional classes. The creative "dimension" can express itself in a cognitive way—through divergent thinking and problem solving—or through the less definable but equally vital "sensing" and intuitive abilities.

Here are some of the benefits of creativity for ELLs, including the gifted:

- **Personal connection.** This is the most significant benefit. ELLs often feel like school is happening to them. Overwhelmed by how much they have to take in, they rarely experience themselves as actors in the process. Creativity and the arts enable them to actively engage in their own learning because they target the individual response—intuiting, reasoning, analyzing, inventing, imagining.
- **Variety of sources and modalities.** Instruction in school tends to be so language-based that the potential of many advanced ELLs is held back by their language development. Creativity and the arts allow them to use different learning styles and modalities to engage in higher-level thinking. They select from a range of activities and material sources that are more adaptable to cultural difference.
- **The possibility of discoveries.** Students love making discoveries, whether they are two or twenty-one. Creativity and the arts provide contexts where advanced ELLs (and all students) encounter something new. Whether it involves composing a poem or proposing a new theory in physics, the creative approach enables gifted Hispanic students to innovate and originate as they may never have before in school.
- **Artistry and feeling.** Some educators may ask, what could be less relevant to learning than artistry and feeling? Artistry and feeling inspire imagination, a key ingredient in most discoveries, inventions, and compositions. In a creative process or arts

activity, students use their keen sensibilities, exploring such phenomena as the intricate patterns in nature, the imagery in poetic verse, or the intensity felt in the dramatization of a historic event. Never underestimate the power of what Rachel Carson (1998) called "the sense of wonder."

To make creativity and the arts a beneficial resource for their classrooms, teachers need to consider their learning goals and how this resource can best advance ELLs and all students. This means identifying areas where units can open up more, knowing the content and skills all students need to acquire, and understanding what creative activities or arts processes can support greater student achievement. Here are some useful questions to consider when preparing to integrate creativity and the arts into specific units or lessons.

- What are the ELL students' learning styles, interests, and special talents?
- What about the other students?
- What should all children understand and be able to do as a result of this class or unit?
- What kind of learning experience makes most sense in this lesson (creative thinking, artistic/imaginative, or sensing/intuiting)?
- Given the above, what kind of adjustment is needed in terms of the level of difficulty, special needs (in language, learning style or skill), the actual process involved, the materials and sources they use?
- How can the arts support a creative activity already in place? For example would a class on photosynthesis benefit from a dramatization? Would collage be an effective catalyst for synthesizing the elements of a story?
- Do the students enjoy moving? Doing things with their hands? Imagining they are someone else? Something else? Somewhere else?
- Which of the arts would best serve the aims and purpose of this specific lesson? What materials?
- In what way would the arts be most effective? As a catalyst in the beginning? As a process throughout the assignment? As a final project?

Creativity presents a much broader range of modalities and thinking styles than the problem-solving models espoused by many schools. Separating divergent thinking, for example, from concerns with artistry and feeling actually can do students a disservice, especially when we consider that real inventors and pioneers often use both. For Nobel Prize winners James Watson and Francis Crick, who had devoted themselves to uncovering the structure of the DNA molecule, intuition rather than hard science led them to conclude that this molecule of life would have to be something beautiful. As they focused on visually striking molecules (like spirals) rather than the more amorphous structures, they discovered their solution. We have to ask, would formal education have allowed the kind of thinking where students relate aesthetics to science or music to language?

Creativity and the arts are not merely enrichment for learning academic subjects. They represent modes of thinking that can fundamentally alter how students understand and relate to knowledge. What different interpretations should be considered from the evidence available? In what ways does the shape of a cube affect how figures look in the paintings of cubists and why? How can dramatizing a historic event change perspective on this event?

In Figure 8.2 is a chart to help you think about creativity and the arts in a different way. The domains presented here are not comprehensive, nor are they separate from each other, as already mentioned.

Figure 8.2　Thinking About Creativity in a Different Way

Sensing/Intuiting	Art Making/Imagining	Knowing/Discovering
• Feeling at a depth level	• Imagining vividly	• Questioning openly
• Having a sense of wonder	• Improvising	• Brainstorming
• Perceiving beyond the surface	• Designing and constructing	• Exploring different points of view
• Intuiting	• Creating images and artwork	• Making meaning
• Daydreaming	• Evoking atmosphere	• Generating many solutions
• Heightened seeing, hearing, or feeling	• Using and responding to visual and performing arts	• Thinking or reasoning divergently
• Visualizing processes and possibilities	• Interpreting	• Associating freely
	• Inventing	• Combining and recombining

We presented the chart in Figure 8.2 to demonstrate that creativity does not confine itself to the cognitive realm, but includes a wider range of sensibilities that we can evoke in the classroom.

Sensing/Intuiting

Keen sensibility is often the first recognizable sign of giftedness in children. Regardless of their cultural or linguistic background, they tend to stand out from the norms of their community by their sensitive responses to the sounds, sights, and sensations around them. These children frequently endure the jibes of friends or family who claim they are too sensitive or who dismiss their empathic responses to the suffering of others. In a world filled with electronic "noise," where children sit for hours in front of screens, the senses become dull and flat. The possibility of surprise escapes them, and nothing they learn transports them from the humdrum round of texting, blogging, and surfing the net. Teachers have a unique opportunity to awaken the senses of all their students and enrich their experience of the world around them. The presence of beauty in the world has a powerful effect on learning.

By beauty we mean a keen awareness and sense of wonder (Carson, 1998) that foster learning through the curiosity it inspires. Children encounter beauty by doing things—exploring, for example, the intricate structure of a molecule, the intriguing vocalizations of birds, or the dazzling array of geometric patterns. They also benefit when you share your own spontaneous and colorful moments—how you choose the scenic routes, brake for animals, and linger over exquisitely prepared French desserts. English language learners know and feel beauty in their culture. Their homes and neighborhoods fill their senses with cooking smells, the rhythms of mariachi and *son* music, colorful fabrics and crafts, and family stories passed down through the generations. This is an essential part of their lived experience and sense of themselves as Spanish-speaking students.

Think about ways to integrate sensing/intuitive activities. Turn the bright lights down so students can listen for a while. Give them different objects to touch (marbles, velvet cushions, bark, stones, gels). Assign homework that requires them to observe, listen, smell, and/or feel. Students from all backgrounds and at all levels love this simple process, and it *teaches* them things and inspires them to want to learn more. Rachel Carson (1998) tells the story of walking through the woods with her grandson, pointing to this or that bird or plant on their way, and discovered that he quickly could distinguish between species and relate details of their living habits.

Here are some ways to ignite the senses:

- The class listens to recorded sounds or those of immediate environment (e.g., school, nature, subway station) and draws, makes collages, designs, or composes sound/musical pieces.
- Assigned homework involves using a sense that is critical in the study of a topic (e.g., observing and recording characteristics of animal species, studying weather changes from feeling temperature and air movement as well as noting thermometer readings).
- The class views and manipulates an object at length, such as moving a radiometer in and out of different light sources, and asks questions, presents options, and sees connections.
- The class explores a number of objects with strong smells and tries to find words to describe them, and (for ELLs and others) assigns colors, shapes, and textures to the smells.
- The class explores ways that senses relate to memories of people, places, things, such the smells of particular foods, products, living things; the sight of particular colors, architecture, clothing; the feel and texture of weather, fabric, musical instruments; and the sound of busy streets, animals, people talking, yelling, laughing, and celebrations.

Very young learners encounter and learn through their senses, and this should remain a part of education, never devalued. Gifted students of all backgrounds tend to get sensory overload due to their heightened sensitivities, so involving them in any process where they can use their senses is a relief and leads them to a special kind of "knowing."

Art Making/Imagining

The arts engage all students, but particularly children from other cultures who need something other than language-based methods of instruction. Goertz (2003) has noted how visual art enhances observation, abstract thinking, and problem analysis. "The artist visualizes and sets goals to find and define the problem, chooses techniques to collect data, and then evaluates and revises the problem solution in order to create" (p. 460). Potentially, the arts enable ELLs to make more meaningful connections to subjects through developing perceptual and analytical skills, kinesthetic understanding, and imagination.

In many ways, the arts bring students back to the world they knew as young children. The joy of discovery returns to them. The arts make numbers, words, and growing things more vivid and alive. Here are some elements of art that teachers can incorporate into units:

- **Line.** The movement between two points either graphically or spatially drawn, such as gradual change in states of one line element or by repetition of line elements. The quality of line that changes from thin to fat, to rough, to wavy, to short, to swift, and tall.
- **Texture.** The changing quality or character or surface from soft, smooth, glossy, waxy, rough, and grained or of a line from dots or short lines.
- **Color.** The property of things seen, such as red, yellow, or blue. Studies developed through relationship, such as opposites and complementary, by attributes such as value, intensity, tint, and shade, and in contextual units such as high value, cool hue; low value, warm hue.

Source: Unit by J. Goertz and K. Arney, in Smutny & von Fremd (2009, p. 260).

Hispanic students with advanced abilities need rich and varied sources to explore. Accelerated instruction will not inspire their souls or respond to their unique sensibilities. More importantly, they will have less opportunity to create a personal relationship with their subjects—something so vital to all learners but especially those who feel foreign or disconnected due to their linguistic or cultural background.

To give you an idea of how you can integrate creativity and the arts, here are some examples.

- Dramatic role-playing to explore point of view and interpret meanings.
- Collage, design, or painting to analyze line, shape, symmetry/asymmetry, or space.
- Composition in rap or "spoken word" about an experience, person, or place.
- Identification with another person (older, younger, different culture, place, living condition), animal (lizard, tiger, salmon, bird), or tree (fir, baobob, weeping willow).

My class went to the arts center and I saw a painting by Remedios Varo. It was called El Paraiso de los Gatos where a cat peeps out of a tower window at other cats outside. Music from Mexico was playing while we looked around. My teacher was saying to me, get into that painting and see what's going on. What's this about and what's that about, she was asking. She had me pick a place in the picture and pretend I was there. I started looking at the cats and the towers and imagined standing on the path right near the tower next to this weird machine thing. Everyone in the class had a painting they looked at. The music kept playing. I felt like I was inside the walls of the tower and next to me was the cat smiling out the window and the green and yellow trees all around me breathing.

—Middle school student

- Creation of a music/sound piece from science (movements of the solar system, the flight patterns of different bird species, the deep forests of Costa Rica).
- Examination of paintings and prints to understand how artists represented concepts of light, shadow, gravity, space, and perspective.
- Creation of a drawing or diagram to represent a mathematical operation.

Knowing/Discovering

Highly creative and resourceful children, including many ELLs, focus much of their energy on discovery and invention, which is why so many struggle when forced to spend a lot of their time on language skills. Creative people, of course, do not follow models in order to do what they do naturally. But knowing these processes can help us identify specific behaviors and how we can support them in the classroom. The most commonly known processes in creative thinking are those identified by Torrance (1979).

Fluency
Focus: generating an abundance of ideas without prejudgment
Process (examples): brainstorming, free association, listing, stream of consciousness

Flexibility
Focus: creating ideas that diverge from the norm

Process (examples): changing, diverging, interpreting, imagining, integrating

Originality
Focus: discovering or producing something unique and individual
Process (examples): generate, compose, inspire, imagine, revise, design, produce

Elaboration
Focus: extending or embellishing on and implementing ideas
Process (examples): analyze, evaluate, synthesize, expand on, determine

In the classroom, open questioning is often the most effective means for guiding children to more creative thinking. It assists ELLs significantly to have key questions posted, as well as different kinds of questions at various levels of difficulty. Some students may hold back or feel unsure, depending on how much experience they have had in creative processes in school. Be sure to provide images, designs, constructions, and the like from different media sources that express the ideas behind the questions. Having the whole class brainstorm together can often give ELLs confidence and creative ideas of their own.

- What are all the facts you know about this idea and what do you not know?
- What are all the different ways you can think of to find out what you need to know?
- What other ways might you design, build, combine, integrate, or reverse?
- What ideas or resources do you feel might relate to what you are doing?
- What could you change in this assignment—materials, process, media—to help you to solve the problem or interpret knowledge and information or discover a new path?

Models of creativity can assist students in sparking their creative powers. For example, in the fluency stage, where the quantity of ideas is the primary aim, teachers can encourage brainstorming (Osborn, 1963). These are the ground rules:

1. Criticism is ruled out (judgment should not interfere with process).

2. Freewheeling is welcomed (wild ideas can become innovative solutions).

3. Quantity is wanted (a long list of possible ideas is the goal).

4. Combination and improvement are sought (ideas in modified or more elaborate form create more options).

In the flexibility and other stages, the SCAMPER method (Stanish, 1988) is useful as well. SCAMPER stands for substitute, combine, adapt, modify-magnify-minify, put to other uses, eliminate, and reverse-rearrange, and teachers can pick and choose what most applies to learning goals and student needs. The method encourages students to think about the different uses of an idea, specific attributes that parallel other ideas (and thereby suggest new uses), and different combinations, rearrangements, and changes that could lead to new, creative ideas.

While there are ample problem solving and thinking strategies, teachers should feel free to pick and choose the parts of a model or strategy that best serve the interests and needs of gifted Hispanic students. A creative process also can draw freely from the visual and performing arts. Divergent thinking, problem solving, and brainstorming invariably work better when they involve art media (visual materials related to the topic at hand, music, drama, video, and so on). Gifted children have active imaginations that are often undernourished without the arts.

Here is an example of how creativity and the arts can support the abilities and needs of an advanced Hispanic ELL.

Fourth grader Jorge was born in the United States, but grew up in a mostly Mexican neighborhood. His first language was Spanish, which both parents speak at home. Because his mother wanted him to have a strong arts program, he applied to and was accepted at a magnet school. He is quiet and withdrawn most of the time, although he relaxes when he can work with other Spanish-speakers. Because of his advanced abilities, Jorge has acquired more English than his peers who started in the same school as he did. He has made exceptional progress in reading over the past year, expresses acuity and perceptiveness verbally, especially in small groups, but becomes frustrated with writing assignments.

What can be done for Jorge?

Let us say you are doing a unit on biography. Students research and write about someone they admire, such as a well-known person (artist, athlete, inventor, scientist), or a relative, adult friend of the family, community leader, or business owner.

Inspire New Ideas

Expose Jorge to different media for telling a life story: film, video, pictures, collage, audio recording, and text. Have him consider how people tell stories about other people he knows: How do they tell it? Do they act it out? Make him laugh, fear, or wonder? Whose story would he like to tell? What does he most want to know about this person? This is his story to tell; what sources and activities does he want to use to tell, show, display, or dramatize his story?

Build on Strengths

Jorge is a visual learner and well-known among his friends for his unique portraits. He also excels at mathematics and design. His father said that at home, he loves to help build things, especially if it involves measuring and calculating shapes. He routinely looks for metal scraps and other objects to construct models for "appliances" he envisions. He also is good at computers, which he taught himself on a laptop belonging to his brother. Jorge would benefit from building on these obvious gifts. He thinks outside the box when he makes his own "appliances," and he would take to an open questioning process in which he feels encouraged to explore any and all options, however outlandish. He loves working with his hands, so he should explore materials he can mold, shape, combine, and so on. His visual learning and Internet research skills enable him to conceptualize his story visually and to find resources (Spanish as well as English) that he needs to supplement text sources at school.

Support Special Needs

Jorge is shy and would benefit from interacting with a partner or small group who could give him the feedback he needs. He loves doing Internet research but needs help organizing his ideas in preparation for writing. When he writes, he spends too much time obsessing over awkward phrases or problems with usage or grammar. Recommendation: Jorge needs to work with a partner or small group when doing assignments that involve writing. He can share what he is interested in finding out, how he plans to do it, and what he has completed. The teacher and other students (the group, or one student if it is a pairing) help him to see the strengths of his work so far and make suggestions on how to address his weaker areas. Since Jorge is a visual learner, he can create a visual design of his story structure (the biography). He can use index cards or a computer program to play with the design (e.g., Where does he want to begin? At the most critical moment of the person's life? What would it look like to work backward from a future time?).

Supplemental Programs for Advanced Hispanic ELLs

Another option for teaching advanced Hispanic ELLs is to create a program *outside* regular school hours. Supplemental programs, while not supplanting school-day offerings, often provide a range of classes in fields not normally studied in school. Typically, students do not have homework (though they may have independent projects they choose to pursue), tests, or grades. Supplemental programs provide a time when "school" is stimulating and fun, when ELLs can learn without pressure, and interact with peers who have similar interests and abilities.

No two programs for the gifted are alike, and that is exactly as it should be. An effective gifted program responds in specific ways to the needs of the community it serves. Those who want to provide services for talented students do not have to go "shopping" for a gifted program and then try to duplicate the model. The knowledge and experiences of schools, institutes, and researchers are important resources, but they should be treated as schematic designs, not blueprints.

Philosophy and Goals

A well-reasoned educational philosophy and clear objectives are essential for an effective program (Smutny, 2003). The philosophy and goals establish the who, what, when, where, why, and how of the gifted program. These form the rationale that parents, teachers, and administrators need to participate in a cohesive way. The philosophy statement maintains the most important focus of the program—the needs, priorities, and values of the population it serves.

In creating the philosophy and goals, program developers should consider these questions:

- What need, situation, circumstance, or observation stimulated the idea for this program?
- What do gifted children most need in this community and what kind of needs assessment has been done to determine this?
- How do community members define talent and ability and what do they most value?

- How do their culture and language affect their views on education and achievement?
- What research on giftedness and gifted education might benefit this community?
- Are there any services for gifted students in this community or district and, if so, do they meet the expectations of the children, parents, administration, and teachers involved?

Effective supplemental programs are no different from school-day programs in requiring well-conceived and clearly stated objectives and courses that offer advanced level instruction through independent, often hands-on learning. Weekend classes, summer workshops, and museum programs can be pivotal experiences for such students. Often these evolve through collaborations among a few of the following: schools, districts, institutes (universities or other educational or cultural organizations), parents, teachers, and community groups. There are no restrictions on the scale of these programs. They can be as simple as a two-Sunday workshop on archeology organized by a handful of parents and teachers or as elaborate as a summer day camp involving hundreds of children from several school districts.

Qualification

It is important that planning begin with the students—in this case, advanced Hispanic ELLs. They determine the criteria used for identification, as well as course design and even assessment. As previous chapters have shown, parents and community members play a key role in any program. In addressing the needs of gifted bilingual students, the Center for Gifted in Illinois reevaluated and redesigned selection procedures, hired bilingual consultants to advise on course content, and developed projects sensitive to their cultural and linguistic differences. The program also used parent consultants, community aides, and bilingual teachers to assist in classrooms when needed.

ELLs of any kind are frequently underrepresented in gifted programs due to unfair selection procedures, particularly the practice of standardized testing. Some students perform well on tests, but most ELLs need additional sources, such as parent or teacher nominations, community members who can vouch for them, portfolios of student work, and in some instances, staff interviews. Criteria should be evenly weighted; that is, test scores should never become the most important measure of ability or achievement.

Class Content

Gifted ELLs need to feel that the program will give them a chance to learn something new without the burden of more writing or reading practice. Furthermore, they need course work that is not packaged for the classroom, but presented in real-world contexts with all the uncertainty and unpredictability that come with it. For example, understanding history by *doing history* reveals the complexity of its process—identifying reliable sources, interpreting evidence, and forming cause-and-effect relationships. The unanswered questions and mysteries in piecing together a history or discovering a pattern in mathematics ignite their imaginations. ELLs can fully participate in these kinds of advanced level classes, as long as they have choices in how they learn and the sources and materials they use.

Programs need to draw on specific cultural values, traditions, and materials to structure content. An excellent example is the Na Pua No'eau program model in Hawaii (Martin, Sing, & Hunter, 2003). *Na Pua* refers to flowers (the children of Hawaii) and *No'eau* to the talents that blossom in the process of self-discovery. This multicultural model integrates Hawaiian ideas about talent and identity development, Hawaiian values and traditions, and the central role of family and community with Western methods of study and enrichment. Gifted students who have benefited from the program find they can advance themselves in subjects such as marine biology, while also exploring their Hawaiian heritage. The cultural dimension of the program increases positive feelings about who they are and what they have to contribute as Hawaiians.

The programs developed through the Center for Gifted respond to the creative needs of gifted children from all cultural, linguistic, and socioeconomic backgrounds. The center makes concerted efforts to reach forgotten communities who rarely receive educational services. Classes emphasize creative thinking in the arts, sciences, and humanities, and offer hands-on activities (e.g., experiments, artwork, inventions, performances, and research projects) that develop students' potential for innovation and discovery. The focus on creativity gives them an alternative to the class work they do in schools.

In the center's intensive three-week project program, classes accommodate advanced ELLs by offering many different modalities for students to process what they are learning. They feature hands-on learning, high mobility between small group and independent work, and projects where students can make discoveries and take more creative risks. An economics class had students assume the roles of business leaders, investors, consumers, and workers through a series of simulations. Over the three weeks, the class grappled with the intriguing relationships between money supply, inflation, the gross national product, the national debt, and unemployment. In a class on mathematical curves, students progressed from an exploration of the simplest circles to the trigonometric function curves and exotic cycloid and spiral curves. Finding curves in spider webs, sound waves, and galaxies, as demonstrated in class activities, inspired many children who would ordinarily avoid abstract mathematics. Having the class explore modern mathematical applications in the Golden Gate Bridge or automobile headlight further expanded course content in meaningful ways. In an aquatic biology class, students tested water samples and researched ecological problems in their areas.

In visual and performing arts classes, students used their creative strengths to design unique art works, plan performances, and explore poetic verse, interpretive movement, and dance. Hispanic ELLs who might cringe before pen and paper assignments, wrote furiously for three weeks in a creative writing class where they responded to a variety of catalysts—films, photographs, paintings, museum exhibits, video works—to create material for poems, stories, and essays. They assembled a 200-page illustrated, creative writing magazine.

Programs need to develop classes that build on the abilities, knowledge, and skills ELLs already have or they will feel overwhelmed by too much new material at one time. The three main points at the beginning of this chapter—*inspire, build* (on strengths), *support* (special needs)—should guide supplemental programs. If classes fail to accommodate linguistic and cultural differences, they cannot engage students who most need exposure to subjects they might never encounter otherwise. Experiences that build on students' cultural strengths and open up the world to them have a significant impact on self-esteem. New interests are born, new talents discovered. Applying their gifts to something in the world (e.g., testing water quality at a local pond, composing a poem for a newspaper) enables them to see themselves differently, which is, in essence, what supplemental programs do best.

Ongoing Assessment

Effective gifted programs are not rigid, nor are they static. A vital program is constantly evolving and responding to changing needs and circumstances. Flexibility is imperative, especially when the participants and their families speak a different language, hold different values, and bring different expectations to the program. Ongoing assessment can head off potential problems and takes a variety of forms: canvassing parents, teachers, and students to see how they feel the program is doing; direct observations by teachers, parents, students, administrators; reviews of student engagement and work; feedback from interpreters, community aides, and families; and fielding questions and concerns voiced by children, parents, support staff, teachers, and administrators. Regular staff meetings also provide a forum for sharing impressions and reports about what is and is not working. The Center for Gifted holds parent seminars that run concurrently with gifted programs, and these provide yet another opportunity to talk with families and share information. The importance of this informal, daily evaluation cannot be overestimated. Without it, problems that could be avoided linger on and become larger issues by the end of the program. Efforts to learn how the program is working send a clear message to families that teachers, staff, and administrators care and are open to change.

A Review of What You Can Do

In this chapter, we explored a number of options for meeting the unique educational needs of advanced Hispanic ELLs. Guiding these options are three key elements: (1) inspiring the imagination; (2) building on strengths; and (3) addressing special language needs. The different approaches described here, such as adjusting the level and pace of instruction, integrating creativity and the arts, and developing supplemental programs, all embrace these three factors in one way or another. Though these factors may seem obvious to some, they are not consistently so, especially for teachers who have to address the most urgent and often different learning needs of the ELLs in their classrooms.

As you ponder what choices will work best for your classroom, consider *your* interests, strengths, and special skills—things you might not normally think of—to create alternatives for advanced ELLs. What do you have to offer from your life experiences, talents, and special skills that could inspire these students? What helpful stories could you tell about your own struggles as a learner? What wisdom could you share about the creative process? What treasured specimens, discoveries, photographs, videos, or artwork can you bring from home to make learning experiences more stimulating and fun? Becoming more aware of the resources you have at your fingertips and the ways you can extend what you are already doing to serve advanced Hispanic ELLs is a practical way to begin your journey.

In designing alternatives for these students, remember that they may present varying levels of language proficiency and require different kinds of support. Make it a priority to discover the abilities and talents of advanced ELLs, taking care not to let language become the filter for your assessment. When selecting any of the options presented in this chapter, consider how the topic and fundamental learning goals lend themselves to particular kinds of adjustments, whether these be accelerated learning options, arts projects, or independent studies. Take these strategies and turn them into something else! Keeping the process open to impromptu teaching moments, unexpected discoveries, and the changing needs of your students means that you can leave the beaten path and make one of your own.

Conclusion

This book has addressed the question of how we can best educate advanced Spanish-speakers in a fair and equitable way. We have adopted a holistic perspective to this question, because improved methods for teaching are not sufficient to address the constellation of needs these students present to schools and classrooms. Through focusing on identification methods, teaching strategies, cultural knowledge, linguistic talents, parent involvement, and community relations, we have shown that including high-potential learners from other cultural and linguistic backgrounds can succeed. But for this inclusion to last, schools need to incorporate all these dimensions. We hope that you can explore each of these elements in your own schools and classrooms.

Identification. Schools need to challenge the deficiency model for teaching ELLs as it tends to narrow the scope of recognized abilities and emphasize remediation. Failing to identify the talents of Spanish-speaking students results in tragedy, not only for them but their communities as well. E. Paul Torrance tells of sixth-grader John Torres, gifted in leadership, art, psychomotor activities, and mechanics, who experienced a radical change in attitude when his school recognized his abilities (Torrance, 1985). He became more alive to the talents within him, took his education more seriously, and progressed rapidly in reading (an area where he was struggling before). A repeated theme throughout this book has been to focus on the abilities of Spanish-speakers. What are their greatest strengths and how do they express them? What life experiences and cultural knowledge can they bring to an independent study project? How do they apply their high mental functioning as interpreters to other academic or creative tasks? This approach to identification creates a far more complete portrait of a child's abilities than standardized tests can ever measure.

Teaching. From this portrait, the child's education begins. It is understandable that teachers feel concerned about the time and resources involved in accommodating Spanish-speakers at the level they require. Yet, as we have shown, providing for their needs demands only incremental changes. One of the messages of this book is to *do what you can with what you have.* In most cases, you can begin by adjusting or expanding on models you already use. Open classroom design, differentiation, SIOP, RtI, creative reasoning, and arts integration—to name a few—are all flexible enough to accommodate advanced Spanish-speakers. Opening up your classrooms to imagination, culture, and creativity, as well as academic learning, enables many ELLs to experience their true gifts for the first time. The results can sometimes be dramatic. Students who appear withdrawn and apathetic often come alive the moment a teacher offers learning options for them to explore and use their talents.

Parent outreach. A key element in working with underserved communities like Spanish-speaking ELLs is to communicate with parents. Many parents fear that their children will lose their culture and language as they become more fluent in English and integrate into American society. We must consider the predicament of parents who sense a cultural cost to success in American schools and who feel they are no longer the primary influence in their children's lives. As explored in this book, welcoming and communicating with parents, expressing respect for their culture, and encouraging them to participate in classrooms (as teaching assistants, interpreters, or professionals) provide opportunities to educate families about the school. Most importantly, teachers and administrators need to honor parents as the students' first teachers and express an openness to embracing cultural knowledge, history, and celebrations in the classroom. In an atmosphere of respect, parents are more likely to participate in the development of programs for advanced Spanish-speakers.

Community relations. Just as important as parent involvement is community outreach. Schools with Spanish-speakers need to become part of the community. This could involve, for example, having administrators and teachers attend local festivals and events; frequent businesses, museums, and community centers; and collaborate with arts groups, musical bands, muralists, and craftsmen—anyone willing to give some time to neighborhood students. Engaging the community in these ways enables schools to learn more about the environment where these children live. It also opens the way for them to secure financial donations or material supplies for underfunded programs that benefit ELLs. Without this commitment to parents and communities, Spanish-speaking learners—even the most gifted—can easily slip through the cracks.

Social and emotional needs. Learning English and attending American schools force non-native-speaking students to think, translate, and interpret between two distinct but overlapping languages and cultures. Advanced learners experience the emotional tug and pull of this process acutely. Teachers can help them achieve a balance between their aspirations in the English-speaking world and their cultural identities as Spanish-speaking Americans. Neglecting this fundamental need may result in highly talented students lowering their expectations because of peer pressure or because their families, who have little connection to the schools, do not fully understand how their children's gifts can benefit them. As mentioned before, communicating with families can noticeably diminish this trend.

Ernesto Bernal (2003) has a forward looking position on bilingualism and multiculturalism in gifted education. It would commit special programs to social as well as academic goals and open the doors to many more communities, including those from Hispanic backgrounds. It would diminish the elitist reputation often associated with gifted education and ignite the imaginations of talented ELLs who feel lost in American schools. Even more, it would enable underserved children to feel at home in a program for advanced learners. Knowing that they belong there immediately would begin to change the way they see themselves and their future in this country.

As teachers and administrators, we do a great service to these children when we nurture and guide the development of their talents. As you listen to them, create with them, and free them to pursue what they do best and most love, we hope that you find the same joy in teaching these special children as we have. We also hope that you experiment with the information we have shared and find your own way to make it work with your students. In our experience, working with advanced Spanish-speaking learners can be a challenging but wondrous adventure. But it is not a journey we can take alone. Uniting with families and communities places us in a much stronger position to ensure lasting benefits for the students who most urgently need them.

Field of hopes
Field of dreams
To me hope is . . .
a flower
growing near a crooked fence
To you hope is . . .
the red robin
whistling a cheery tune
(as joyful as can be)
My dream?
To walk through nature
as gently as a tiger with her cubs
Yours?
To snap a photo
of a rainbow you saw today
Never let your hopes be broken
Never let someone squash your dreams
Be free
Be joyful
Be you.

—Estrella, Grade 5

Appendix

Organizations and Publishers

California Association for the Gifted (www.cagifted.org)

Website for the California Association for the Gifted.

Center for the Gifted (www.centerforgifted.org)

The Center for the Gifted, a Northern Illinois University partner, focuses on offering programs for gifted students. They cater to the interests and intelligence levels of students.

Center for Talent Development (www.ctd.northwestern.edu)

Center for Talent Development (CTD), housed at Northwestern University's School of Education and Social Policy.

Council for Exceptional Children (www.cec.sped.org)

The Council for Exceptional Children (CEC) is the largest international professional organization focused on improving the educational experience for students with disabilities or gifts and talents.

Davidson Academy of Nevada (www.davidsonacademy.unr .edu)

The Davidson Academy of Nevada is a public school for profoundly gifted students. While grade levels are not identified, middle and high school students can attend.

Davidson Institute (www.davidsongifted.org)

A national nonprofit organization dedicated to supporting profoundly gifted students under the age of 18. This foundation provides guidance for students who score in the 99.9th percentile on IQ and achievement tests.

EPGY: The Education Program for Gifted Youth (epgy.stanford.edu)

The Education Program for Gifted Youth (EPGY) at Stanford University offers on-line educational experiences targeted at high-ability students.

Equity in Gifted/Talented (G/T) Education (www.gtequity.org/connecting.php)

The goal of the Equity in Gifted/Talented Education project is to encourage equitable representation of student populations in G/T programs throughout the state.

Gifted Students Institute (smu.edu/education/gsi)

Southern Methodist University of Texas offers support for working with gifted students. They host courses for teachers of gifted.

Great Potential Press (www.greatpotentialpress.com)

Great Potential Press brings quality books and materials to parents and educators of gifted students. They offer some materials published in Spanish.

GT World (gtworld.org)

GT World is an online community where educators and parents can find support, references, and guidance as they work with gifted students.

Hoagies' Gifted Education Page (hoagiesgifted.org)

Hoagies' Gifted Education Page is the "All Things Gifted" resource for parents, educators, administrators, counselors, psychologists, and even gifted kids and teens themselves!

International Baccalaureate (www.ibo.org)

The International Baccalaureate (IB) is a nonprofit educational foundation. IB offers support for working with their three programs designed for gifted students aged 3 to 19.

Ignite Creative Learning Studio (www.ignitecreativelearning .com)

Ignite Creative Learning Studio, located in Ojai, California, is a dynamic educational learning laboratory and think tank dedicated to the practical application of creativity, problem solving, and gifted education best practices to academic subjects, including math, language arts, science, and history.

National Association for Gifted Children (www.nagc.org)

Website for the National Association for Gifted Children.

National Association of Parents With Children in Special Education (www.napcse.org/exceptionalchildren/giftedan-dtalented.php)

A place where parents of children in special education can find everything they need to know to be their child's best advocate.

National Society for the Gifted & Talented (nsgt.org)

The National Society for the Gifted & Talented provides guidance and references for connecting gifted and talented youth with opportunities based on their interests and high abilities.

State Associations and State Departments for the Gifted and Talented (www.nsgt.org/resources/state.asp)

This site of the National Society for the Gifted & Talented (NSGT) contains further links to state associations and departments for the gifted and talented.

National Associations for Gifted and Talented Students (www.nsgt.org/resources/national_associations.asp)

This portion of the National Society for the Gifted and Talented (NSGT) web site provides direct links to organizations involved in promoting gifted and talented education.

Neag Center for Gifted Education and Talent Development (www.gifted.uconn.edu)

Web site for the University of Connecticut, home to the Neag Center for Gifted Education and Talent Development. At the very end of a lengthy list of recourses is a list of references available in Spanish.

NSW Association for Gifted & Talented Children (nswagtc .org.au)

This is an open association (incorporated in the state of New South Wales, Australia) for educators and parents. The web site offers information on advocating for gifted and talented services.

Prufrock Press (www.prufrock.com)

Prufrock Press offers award-winning products focused on gifted education, gifted children, advanced learning, and special needs learners.

Summer Institute for the Gifted (www.giftedstudy.org)

The Summer Institute for the Gifted offers residential and day programs for gifted and talented students of ages 4 through 17.

Supporting Emotional Needs of the Gifted (www.sengifted .org)

Supporting Emotional Needs of the Gifted (SENG) is a non-profit organization that provides support and resources to educators and parents. They focus on nurturing the social and emotional needs of the gifted.

Talento y Educación (www.javiertouron.es/)

Javier Tourón is a professor in Spain who started this blog on gifted education.

Texas Association for the Gifted and Talented (www.txgifted .org)

The Texas Association for the Gifted and Talented (TAGT) is an organization focused on providing support and resources to those who work with gifted students. It is the largest organization of its kind in the nation.

2e: Twice-Exceptional Newsletter (www.2enewsletter.com)

One of the few publications focused directly on twice-exceptional children—those who are exceptional because they are gifted and because they have learning disabilities.

Books and Articles

American Association for Gifted Children. (1978). *On being gifted*. New York: Walker.

Brown, C. L. (2004). Reducing the over-referral of culturally and linguistically diverse students (CLD) for language disabilities. *NABE Journal of Research and Practice, 2*(1), 225–243. Retrieved from http://njrp.tamu.edu/2004/PDFs/Brown.pdf

Bruch, C. B. (1975). Assessment of creativity in culturally different children. *Gifted Child Quarterly, 19*(2), 164–174.

Calderón, M., Slavin, R., & Sanchez, M. (2011). Effective instruction for English learners. *The Future Child, 21*(1), 103–127.

California Association for the Gifted. (1999). *Advocating for gifted English language learners: An activity handbook for professional development and self-study.* Los Angeles: California Association for the Gifted.

Castellano, J. A., & Frazier, A. D. (2010). *Special populations in gifted education.* Waco, TX: Prufrock Press.

Coil, C. (2002). *Practical tips for parents—Consejos practicos para los padres.* Dayton, OH: Pieces of Learning.

Colangelo, N. Assouline, S. G., & Gross, M. U. M. (2004). *Una nación engañada.* Retrieved from www.accelerationinstitute.org/Nation_Deceived/Get_Report.aspx

Delisle, J., & Galbraith, J. (2002). *When gifted kids don't have all the answers: How to meet their social and emotional needs.* Minneapolis: Free Spirit.

Donovan, M. S., & Cross, C. T. (Eds). (2002). *Minority students in special and gifted education.* Washington, DC: National Academy Press.

Ford, D. Y., & Milner, H. R. (2005). *Teaching culturally diverse gifted students.* Waco, TX: Prufrock Press.

Frasier, M. M., Hunsaker, S. L., Lee, J., Mitchell, S., Cramond, B., Krisel, S., . . . Finley, V. S. (1995). *Core attributes of giftedness: A foundation for recognizing the gifted potential of minority and economically disadvantaged students.* Storrs, CT: National Research Center on the Gifted and Talented.

Frasier, M. M., Martin, D., García, J. H., Finley, V. S., Frank, E., Krisel, S., & King, L. L. (1995). *A new window for looking at gifted children.* Storrs, CT: National Research Center on the Gifted and Talented.

Galbraith, J. (1999). *The gifted kids' survival guide.* Minneapolis: Free Spirit.

Galbraith, J., & Delisle, J. (1987). *The gifted kids' survival guide II.* Minneapolis: Free Spirit.

Gándara, P. (2005). *Latino achievement: Identifying models that foster success.* Storrs, CT: National Research Center for the Gifted and Talented.

Harry, B., & Klingner, J. (2006). *Why are so many minority students in special education? Understanding race and disability in schools.* New York: Teachers College Press.

Hawkins, W. A. (1995). *Constructing a secure mathematics pipeline for minority students.* Washington: University of the District of Columbia.

Heacox, D. (2002). *Differentiating instruction in the regular classroom.* Minneapolis: Free Spirit.

Hine, C. Y. (1994). *Helping your child find success at school: A Guide for Hispanic parents.* Storrs: University of Connecticut.

Hine, C. Y. (1994). *Cómo ayudar a su hijo a tener exito en la escuela: Guía para padres hispanos,* Storrs: University of Connecticut.

Hollingworth, L. S. (1942). *Children above 180 I.Q.: Stanford Binet.* Yonkers-on-Hudson, NY: World Book.

Hunsaker, S. L., Frasier, M. M., King, L. L., Watts-Warren, B., Cramond, B., & Krisel, S. (1995). *Family influences on the achievement of economically disadvantaged students: Implications for gifted identification and programming.* Athens: University of Georgia.

Jolly, J. L., Treffinger, D. J., Inman, T. F., & Smutny, J. F. (Eds.). (2011). *Parenting gifted children.* Waco, TX: Prufrock Press.

Kitano, M. K., & Pedersen, K. S. (2002). Action research and practical inquiry: Teaching gifted English learners. *Journal for the Education of the Gifted, 26*(2), 132–147.

Kloosterman, V. I. (1999). *Socio-cultural contexts for talent development: A qualitative study on high ability, Hispanic, bilingual students.* Storrs, CT: National Research Center on the Gifted and Talented.

Lohman, D. F. (2005). *Identifying academically talented minority students,* Iowa City: University of Iowa.

Matthews, D., Foster, J., Gladstone, D., Schieck, J., & Meiners, J. (2007). Supporting professionalism, diversity, and context within a collaborative approach to gifted education. *Journal of Educational and Psychological Consultation, 17*(4), 315–345.

Matthews, M. S. (2006). *Working with gifted English language learners.* Waco, TX: Prufrock Press.

Moon, T., Tomlinson, C. A., & Callahan, C. M. (1995). *Academic diversity in the middle school: Results of a national survey of middle school administrators and teachers.* Storrs, CT: National Research Center on the Gifted and Talented.

National Association for Gifted Children. (2011). *Javits program supports high-ability learners from underrepresented populations.* Retrieved from http://www.nagc.org/uploadedFiles/PDF/Advocacy_PDFs/Javits%20-%20 underrep%20pops.pdf

Newland, T. E. (1976). *The gifted in socioeducational perspective.* Englewood Cliffs, NJ: Prentice Hall.

Oakland, T., & Rossen, E. (2005, October). A 21st-century model for identifying students for gifted and talented programs in light of national conditions: An emphasis on race and ethnicity. *Gifted Child Today, 28*(4), 56–63.

Runco, M. A., & Pritzker, S. R. (1999). *Encyclopedia of creativity, volume 1*. Salt Lake City, UT: Academic Press.

Smutny, J. F., & von Fremd, S. E. (2010). *Differentiating for the young child* (2nd ed.). Thousand Oaks, CA: Corwin.

Smutny, J. F., Walker, S. Y., & Meckstroth, E. A. (2007). *Acceleration for gifted learners*. Thousand Oaks, CA: Corwin.

Tomlinson, C. A., Callahan, C. M., Moon, T., Tomchin, E. M., Landrum, M., Imbeau, M., . . . & Eiss, N. (1995). *Preservice teacher preparation in meeting the needs of gifted and other academically diverse students*. Storrs, CT: National Research Center on the Gifted and Talented.

Trumbull, E., Rothstein-Fisch, C., Greenfield, P., & Quiroz, B. (2001). *Bridging cultures between home and school: A guide for teachers*. Mahwah, NJ: Erlbaum.

Valdés, G. (2002). *Understanding the special giftedness of young interpreters*. Storrs, CT: National Research Center on the Gifted and Talented.

Whitmore, J. R. (1980). *Giftedness, conflict and underachievement*. Boston: Allyn & Bacon.

Winebrenner, S. (2001). *Teaching gifted kids in the regular classroom: Strategies and techniques every teacher can use to meet the academic needs of the gifted and talented*. Minneapolis: Free Spirit.

Resources for the Classroom

Byrdseed.com (www.byrdseed.com)

Colorín Colorado (www.colorincolorado.org)

J. Taylor Education (www.jtayloreducation.org)

Legacy Station Educational-Game Toys (www.legacystation .com/EduGames.htm)

The Math League (www.themathleague.com)

Cultural Books for the K–3 Classroom

Ada, Alma F., & Elivia Savadier. (2004). *I love Saturdays y domingos*. New York: Atheneum Books.

Ada, Alma F., & Gabriel M. Zubizarreta. (2011). *Dancing home*. New York: Atheneum Books.

Altman, Linda J., & Enrique O. Sanchez. (1995). *Amelia's road*. New York: Lee & Low.

Baca, Ana, Anthony Accardo, & Jose J. Coin. (2003). *Chiles for Benito/Chiles para Benito*. Houston, TX: Piñata Books.

Brown, Monica, & Sara Palacios. (2011). *Marisol McDonald doesn't match/ Marisol McDonald no combina*. New York: Children's Book Press.

Climo, Shirley, & Francisco Mora. (1999). *Little red ant and the great big crumbs: A Mexican fable*. Boston: Sandpiper.

Conkling, Winifred. (2011). *Sylvia & Aki*. Berkeley, CA: Tricycle Press.

González, Lucia M., & Lulu Delacre. (1999). *The bossy Gallito*. New York: Scholastic.

Gonzalez, Ralfka, & Ana Ruiz. (1995). *Mi primer libro de dichos* (My first book of proverbs). San Francisco: Children's Book Press.

Hayes, Joe, & Antonio L. Castro. (2008). *Gum-chewing rattler*. El Paso, TX: Cinco Puntos Press.

Jiménez, Francisco. (2000). *La mariposa*. Boston: Sandpiper.

Jules, Jaqueline, & Miguel Bernítez. (2012). *Zapata power*. Park Ridge, IL: Albert Whitman.

Kimmel, Eric A., & Valerie Docampo. (2009). *The three little tamales*. Whitestown, IN: Amazon Children's Publishing.

Krull, Kathy, & Yuyi Morales. (2003). *Harvesting hope: The story of Cesar Chavez*. Boston: Harcourt.

Laínez, Rene C. (2010). *My shoes and I*. Honesdale, PA: Boyds Mills Press.

Laínez, Rene C. (2010). *Tooth fairy meets El Ratón Pérez*. Berkeley, CA: Tricycle Press.

McDermott, Gerald. (1999). *Coyote: A trickster tale from the American southwest*. Boston: Sandpiper.

Medina, Meg, & Claudio Muñoz. (2011). *Tía Isa wants a car*. New York: Candlewick Press.

Montes, Marisa, & Yuyi Morales. (2006). *Los gatos black on Halloween*. New York: Henry Holt.

Mora, Pat, & Raul Colón. (2000). *Tómas and the library lady*. New York: Dragonfly Books.

Reiser, Lynn. (1996). *Margaret and Margarita/Margarita y Margaret*. New York: Greenwillow.

Sáenz, Benjamin A., & Geronimo Garcia. (2009). *The dog who loved tortillas/La perrita que le encantaban las tortillas*. El Paso, TX: Cinco Puntos Press.

Schachner, Judy. (2011). *Skippyjon Jones*. New York: Puffin.

Soto, Gary. (1996). *Too many tamales*. New York: Puffin.

Stevens, Jan R., & Jeanne Stevens. (1995). *Carlos and the squash plant*. Lanham, MD: Cooper Square.

Tonatiuh, Duncan. (2010). *Dear primo: A letter to my cousin*. New York: Abrams Books.

Vamos, Samantha R., & Rafael López. (2011). *Cazuela that the farm maiden stirred*. Watertown, MA: Charlesbridge.

Cultural Books for the 4–5 Classroom

Alvarez, Julia. (2010). *Return to sender*. New York: Yearling.

Beatty, Patricia. (2000). *Lupita mañana*. New York: HarperCollins.

Deedy, Carmen A., & Michael Austin. (2008). *Martina the beautiful cockroach*. Atlanta: Peachtree.

Gallagher, Diane. (2010). *Claudia Cristina Cortez uncomplicates your life*. North Mankato, MN: Stone Arch.

Hayes, Joe, Vickie T. Hill, & Mona Pennypacker. (2006). *La llorona/The weeping woman*. El Paso, TX: Cinco Puntos Press.

Jiménez, Francisco. (1997). *The circuit*. Albuquerque: University of New Mexico Press.

Jiménez, Francisco. (2002). *Breaking through*. Boston: Sandpiper.

Jiménez, Francisco. (2008). *Reaching out*. Boston: Houghton Mifflin.

Resau, Laura. (2010). *Star in the forest*. New York: Delacorte Books.

Ryan, Pam M. (2002). *Esperanza rising*. New York: Scholastic.

Ryan, Pam M. (2005). *Becoming Naomi León*. New York: Scholastic.

Soto, Gary. (2000). *Baseball in April and other stories*. Boston: Sandpiper.

Cultural Books for the 6–7+ Classroom

Canfield, Jack, Mark V. Hansen, & Susan Sanchez-Casal. (2005). *Chicken soup for the Latino soul: Celebrating la comunidad latina*. Deerfield Beach, FL: HCI.

McCall, Guadalupe G. (2011). *Under the mesquite*. New York: Lee & Low Books.

McDougall, Christopher. (2011). *Born to run: A hidden tribe, superathletes, and the greatest race the world has never seen*. New York: Vintage.

Nava, Yolanda. (2000). *It's all in the frijoles: 100 famous latinos share real-life stories*. Lady Lake, FL: Fireside.

Pérez, L. King, & Robert Casilla. (2002). *First day in grapes*. New York: Lee & Low Books.

Resau, Laura, & Maria V. Farinango. (2012). *The queen of water*. New York: Ember.

Bibliography

Aguila, V. (2010). *Improving education for English learners: Research-based approaches.* Sacramento: California Department of Education. Retrieved from http://www.sccoe.org/depts/ell/accountability/11thannual/VeronicaAguilaAccountability%202010.ppt

Ames, C. A. (1990). Motivation: What teachers need to know. *Teachers College Record, 91*(3), 409–421.

Anderson, L. W., & Krathwohl, D. R. (Eds.). (2001). *A taxonomy for learning, teaching, and assessing: A revision of Bloom's taxonomy of educational objectives.* New York: Longman.

Armstrong, T. (2002). *You're smarter than you think: A kid's guide to multiple intelligences.* Minneapolis: Free Spirit.

Aud, S., Fox, M. A., & KewalRamani, A. (2010). *Status and trends in the education of racial and ethnic groups.* Washington, DC: U.S. Department of Education, National Center for Education Statistics. Retrieved from http://nces.ed.gov/pubs2010/2010015.pdf

Baldwin, A. Y. (2003). Lost and found: Achievers in urban schools. In J. Smutny (Ed.), *Underserved gifted populations: Responding to their needs and abilities* (pp. 83–91). Cresskill, NJ: Hampton Press.

Barstow, D. (1987). Serve disadvantaged and serve all gifted. *Gifted Child Monthly, 8*(10), 1–3.

Beacham, H. C. (1980). *Reaching and helping high school dropouts and potential school leavers.* (ERIC Document Reproduction Service No. ED 236451). Tallahassee: Florida A&M University.

Bernal, E. M. (1981, February). *Special problems and procedures for identifying minority gifted students.* Paper presented at the Council for Exceptional Children Conference on the Exceptional Bilingual Child, New Orleans, LA.

Bernal, E. M. (2003). Delivering two-way bilingual immersion programs to gifted and talented: A classic yet progressive option for the new millennium. In J. F. Smutny (Ed.), *Underserved gifted populations: Responding to their needs and abilities* (pp. 141–156). Cresskill, NJ: Hampton Press.

Blume, H. (2010, May 9). L.A. schools on sharper lookout for gifted students—and they find them. *Los Angeles Times.* Retrieved from http://articles.latimes.com/2010/may/09/local/la-me-0509-gifted-20100509

Brighton, C. M., Moon, T., Jarvis, J., & Hockett, J. (2007). *Primary grade teachers' conceptions of giftedness and talent: A case-based investigation.* Storrs: National Research Center on the Gifted and Talented, University of Connecticut.

Brown, C. L. (2004). Content based ESL curriculum and academic language proficiency. *The Internet TESL Journal, 10*(2). Retrieved from http://iteslj.org/Techniques/Brown-CBEC.html

California Association for the Gifted. (1999). *Advocating for gifted English language learners: An activity handbook for professional development and self-study.* (English and Spanish versions.) Los Angeles: California Association for the Gifted.

California Department of Education. (2009a). *Gifted and talented education enrollment 2008–09 state of California* (data set). Retrieved from http://dq.cde.ca.gov/dataquest/DQ/GateStudents.aspx?ReportCode=StGate&CountyCode=00&DistrictCode=00000&SchoolCode=0000000&TheYear=2008–09&Level=State

California Department of Education. (2009b). *Special education enrollment by ethnicity and disability statewide report* (data set).

Callahan, C. M. (2005). Identifying gifted students from underrepresented populations. *Theory Into Practice, 44*(2), 98–104. Retrieved from http://findarticles.com/p/articles/mi_m0NQM/is_2_44/ai_n13783926/

Carson, R. (1998). *A sense of wonder.* (N. Kelsh, Photo.). New York: Harper Collins.

Caspi, A., Wright, B. E., Moffit, T. E., & Silva, P. A. (1998). Childhood predictors of unemployment in early adulthood. *American Sociological Review, 63*(3), 424–451.

Castellano, J. A. (1998). *Identifying and assessing gifted and talented bilingual Hispanic students* (Eric Digest, ED423104). Charleston, WV: ERIC Clearinghouse on Rural Education and Small Schools. Retrieved from http://www.eric.ed.gov/PDFS/ED423104.pdf

Center for Comprehensive School Reform and Improvement. (2005, August). *Meeting the challenge: Getting parents involved in schools.* Retrieved from http://www.centerforcsri.org

Cisneros, S. (1991). *The house on Mango Street.* New York: Vintage Books. (Original work published 1984)

Cisneros, S. (2009). *Sandra Cisneros: Early life video interview.* Knopf Group. Retrieved from http://www.youtube.com/watch?v=4CuRcFkH9nU

Clark, B. (2007). Issues of identification and underrepresentation. *Gifted Education Communicator, 38*(1), 22–25.

Cook, N. A., Wittig, C. V., & Treffinger, D. J. (2011). The path from potential to productivity: The parent's role in the levels of service approach to talent development. In J. L. Jolly, D. J. Treffinger, T. F. Inman, & J. F. Smutny (Eds.), *Parenting gifted children* (pp. 243–257). Waco, TX: Prufrock Press.

Cooper, C. R. (2008). The school's role in parenting gifted students. *Gifted Education Communicator, 39*(2), 9–11.

Cummins, J. (1979) Cognitive/academic language proficiency, linguistic interdependence, the optimum age question and some other matters. *Working Papers on Bilingualism, 19,* 121–129.

Cummins, J. (1981). The role of primary language development in promoting educational success for language minority students. In California State Department of Education (Ed.), *Schooling and language minority students: A theoretical framework* (pp. 3–49). Los Angeles: Evaluation, Dissemination and Assessment Center, California State University.

Delisle, J., & Galbraith, J. (2002). *When gifted kids don't have all the answers: How to meet their social and emotional needs.* Minneapolis: Free Spirit.

DeVries, A. R. (2011). Productive parent teacher conferences. In J. L. Jolly, D. J. Treffinger, T. F. Inman, & J. F. Smutny (Eds.), *Parenting gifted children* (pp. 316–321). Waco, TX: Prufrock Press.

Echevarria, J., Vogt, M., & Short, D. J. (2004). *Making content comprehensible for English language learners: The SIOP model* (2nd ed.). Boston: Allyn & Bacon.

English-language learners. (2011, August 10), *Education Week.* Retrieved from http://www.edweek.org/ew/issues/english-language-learners/

Fillmore, L. W. (2000). Loss of family languages: Should educators be concerned? Children and languages at school and languages at school. *Theory Into Practice, 39*(4), 203–210.

Fry, R. (2011, August). *Hispanic college enrollment spikes, narrowing gaps with other groups.* Washington, DC: Pew Hispanic Center. Retrieved from http://www.pewhispanic.org/2011/08/25/hispanic-college-enrollment-spikes-narrowing-gaps-with-other-groups/

Galeano, E. (1993). *Walking words* (J. F. Borges, Illus.). New York: W.W. Norton.

Gallagher, R. M. (2007). Nurturing global citizens for the 21st century. *Understanding Our Gifted, 20*(1), 7–11.

Gándara, P., & Contreras, F. (2009). *The Latino education crisis: The consequences of failed social policies.* Cambridge, MA: Harvard University Press. Retrieved from http://www.nea.org/home/17404.htm

Gardner, H. (1983). *Frames of mind: The theory of multiple intelligences.* New York: Basic Books.

Gardner, H. (1999). *Intelligence reframed: Multiple intelligences for the 21st century.* New York: Basic Books.

Getzels, J., & Jackson, P. (1962). *Creativity and intelligence.* New York: John Wiley.

Goertz, J. (2003). Searching for talent through the visual arts. In J. F. Smutny (Ed.), *Underserved gifted populations: Responding to their needs and abilities* (pp. 459–467). Cresskill, NJ: Hampton Press.

González, N., Moll, L. C., & Amanti, C. (Eds.). (2005). *Funds of knowledge: Theorizing practiced in households, communities, and classrooms.* Mahwah, NJ: Erlbaum.

Guilford, J. P. (1950). Creativity. *American Psychologist, 5*(9), 444–454.

Harvard University. (2002). *What works for the children? What we know and don't know about bilingual education.* The Civil Rights Project. Cambridge, MA: Harvard University.

Haynes, J., & Zacarian, D. (2010). *Teaching English language learners across the content areas.* Alexandria, VA: Association for Supervision and Curriculum Development.

Heacox, D. (2002). *Differentiating instruction in the regular classroom: How to reach and teach all learners, grades 3–12.* Minneapolis: Free Spirit.

Henderson, A. T., & Berla, N. (1995). *A new generation of evidence: Family is critical to student achievement.* Washington, DC: Center for Law and Education.

Hill, J., & Björk, C. (2008). *Classroom instruction that works with English language learners: Facilitator's guide.* Alexandria, VA: Association for Supervision and Curriculum Development.

Hopstock, P. J., & Stephenson, T. G. (2003). *Descriptive study of services to LEP students and LEP students with disabilities: Special topic report #2.* Analysis of Office of Civil Rights data related to LEP students. Washington, DC: U.S. Department of Education, Office of English Language Acquisition.

Hurley, P. (2010). Academic language: Equipping English learners to speak and write confidently in secondary classrooms. *Gifted Education Communicator, 41*(4), 21–25.

Jiménez, F. (1997). *The circuit: Stories from the life of a migrant child.* New York: Houghton Mifflin.

Krashen, S. D. (1982). *Principles and practice in second language acquisition.* Oxford, UK: Pergamon Press. Retrieved from http://www.sdkrashen.com/Principles_and_Practice/Principles_and_Practice.pdf

Krashen, S. D. (2004). *The power of reading: Insights from the research* (2nd ed.). Englewood, CO: Libraries Unlimited.

Krashen, S. D., & Brown, C. L. (2007). What is academic language proficiency? *STETS Language & Communication Review, 6*(1), 1–3. Retrieved from http://www.sdkrashen.com/articles/Krashen_Brown_ALP.pdf

Krashen, S. D., & Terrell, T. D. (1983). *The natural approach: Language acquisition in the classroom.* London: Prentice Hall Europe.

Little, S. F., & Kaesberg, M. A. (2011). Increasing the eligibility of Title I students for gifted education programs: Pilot study using the Kingore Observation Inventory. *Gifted Education Press Quarterly, 25*(3), 9–14.

Lochner, L., & Moretti, E. (2004). The effect of education on crime: Evidence from prison inmates, arrests, and self reports. *The American Economic Review, 94*(1), 155–189.

Marland, S. P., Jr. (1972). *Education of the gifted and talented: Report to the Congress of the United States by the U.S. Commissioner of Education and background papers submitted to the U.S. Office of Education,* 2 vols. (Government Documents Y4.L 11/2: G36).Washington, DC: U.S. Government Printing Office.

Martin, D. E., Sing, D. K., & Hunter, L. (2003). Na pua no'eau: The Hawaiian perspective of giftedness. In J. F. Smutny (Ed.), *Underserved gifted populations: Responding to their needs and abilities* (pp. 179–203). Cresskill, NJ: Hampton Press.

Marzano, R., & Pickering, D. (2005). *Building academic vocabulary: Teacher's manual.* Alexandria, VA: Association for Supervision and Curriculum Development.

Maslow, A. H. (1968). *Toward a psychology of being* (2nd ed.). New York: D. Van Nostrand.

May, R. (1975). *The courage to create.* New York: W.W. Norton.

Mendoza, J. (2005, July). *Cultural awareness.* Presentation at ACSA's Principal Summer Institute, Los Angeles: University of California at Los Angeles.

Moll, L. C. (Ed.). (1990). *Vygotsky and education: Instructional implications and applications of sociohistorical psychology.*: Cambridge: Cambridge University Press.

Moll, L. C. (1992). Funds of knowledge for teaching: Using a qualitative approach to connect homes and classrooms. *Theory Into Practice, 31*(2), 132–141.

National Association for Gifted Children. (2008). *NAGC position statements: Competencies needed by teachers.* Retrieved from http://www.nagc.org/index.aspx?id=385

National Association for Gifted Children. (2011a). Giftedness among underserved and disadvantaged populations. *NAGC message.* Retrieved from http://www.nagc.org/uploadedFiles/News_Room/NAGC_Advocacy_in_the_News/NAGC%20MESSAGES%20(for%20website).pdf

National Association for Gifted Children. (2011b). *What is giftedness?* Retrieved from http://www.nagc.org/index.aspx?id=574&terms=definitions+of+gifted

National Center for Children's Illustrated Literature. (2008). *David Diaz.* Abilene, TX: National Center for Children's Illustrated Literature. Retrieved from http://nccil.org/experience/artists/diazd/index.htm

National Center for Education Statistics. (2009a). *Number and percentage of children served under Individuals with Disabilities Education Act, Part B, by age group and state or jurisdiction: Selected years, 1990–91 through 2008–09,* Table 47. Washington, DC: U.S. Department of Education. Retrieved from http://nces.ed.gov/programs/digest/d10/tables/dt10_047.asp

National Center for Education Statistics. (2009b). *Percentage of public school 4th-graders eligible for free or reduced-price lunch, by school locale and race/ethnicity: 2009,* Table 7.5a. Washington, DC: U.S. Department of Education. Retrieved from http://nces.ed.gov/pubs2010/2010015/tables/table_7_5a.asp

National Center for Education Statistics. (2010a). Children 3 to 21 years old served under Individuals with Disabilities Education Act, Part B, by type of disability: Selected years, 1976–77 through 2008–09, Table 45. *Digest of Education Statistics.* Washington, DC: U.S. Department of Education. Retrieved from http://nces.ed.gov/programs/digest/d10/tables/dt10_045.asp?referrer=list

National Center for Education Statistics. (2010b). High-poverty schools. *The condition of education 2010.* (NCES 2010–028). Washington, DC: U.S. Department of Education. Retrieved from http://nces.ed.gov/pubs2010/2010028.pdf

National Center for Education Statistics. (2010c). Percentage of high school dropouts among persons 16 through 24 years old (status dropout rate), by sex and race/ethnicity: Selected years, 1960 through 2009, Table 115. *Digest of Education Statistics.* Washington, DC: U.S. Department of Education. Retrieved from http://nces.ed.gov/programs/digest/d10/tables/dt10_115.asp

National Center for Education Statistics. (2011). *The condition of education 2011.* (NCES 2011–033) Indicator 20. Washington, DC: U.S. Department of Education. Retrieved from http://nces.ed.gov/pubs2011/2011034.pdf

National Clearinghouse. (2000). *Why is it important to maintain the native language?* IDRA Newsletter, Author. Retrieved from http://www.idra.org/IDRA_Newsletter/January_2000_Bilingual_Edu

National Clearinghouse for English Language Acquisition. (2008). English learners served under IDEA Part B, by state, 2008. *ELs with special needs: National overview.* Washington, DC: National Clearinghouse for English Language Acquisition.

National Education Association. (2007). *Truth in labeling: Disproportionality in special education.* NEA report. Retrieved from http://www.nccrest.org/Exemplars/Disporportionality_Truth_In_Labeling.pdf

National Research Center on Learning Disabilities. (2007). *SLD identification overview.* NRCLD report. Retrieved from http://www.nrcld.org/resource_kit/tools/SLDOverview2007.pdf

Nava, Y. (2000). *It's all in the frijoles.* New York: Fireside.

Nieto, S., & Bode, P. (2008). *Affirming diversity: The sociopolitical context of multicultural education* (5th ed.) Boston: Pearson Education.

North Central Regional Educational Laboratory. (1994). Funds of knowledge: A look at Luis Moll's research into hidden family resources. *Cityschools, 1*(1), 19–21.

Oregon Department of Education. (2010). *Statewide report card 2009–10.* Retrieved from http://www.ode.state.or.us/data/annreportcard/rptcard2010.pdf

Osborn, A. F. (1963). *Applied imagination* (3rd ed.). New York: Scribner.

Payán, R., & Nettles, M. (2006). *Current state of English language learners in the U.S. K–12 student population.* ELL Factsheet. Retrieved from http://www.ets.org/Media/Conferences_and_Events/pdf/ELLsymposium/ELL_factsheet.pdf

Peterson, J. S. (2011). A counselor's perspective on parenting for high potential. In J. L. Jolly, D. J. Treffinger, T. F. Inman, & J. F. Smutny (Eds.), *Parenting gifted children* (pp. 525–538). Waco, TX: Prufrock Press.

Pew Hispanic Center. (2009, December). *Between two worlds: How young Latinos come of age in America.* Washington, DC: Pew Hispanic Center. Retrieved from http://www.pewhispanic.org/files/reports/117.pdf

Pew Hispanic Center. (2011, July). *The Mexican-American boom: Births overtake immigration.* Washington, DC: Pew Hispanic Center. Retrieved from http://pewhispanic.org/files/reports/144.pdf

President's Commission on Excellence in Special Education. (2002). *A new era: Revitalizing special education for children and their families.* Jessup, MD: ED Pubs.

Renzulli, J., & Park, S. (2000). Gifted dropouts: The who and the why. *Gifted Child Quarterly, 44*(4), 261–271.

Rimm, S. (2008). *Why bright kids get poor grades and what you can do about it.* Scottsdale, AZ: Great Potential Press.

Robertson, K. (2006). *Increasing academic language knowledge for English language learner success.* Arlington, VA: Colorín Colorado. Retrieved from http://www.colorincolorado.org/article/13347/

Robinson, K. (2009). *The element: How finding your passion changes everything.* New York: Viking.

Rogers, C. (1970). Towards a theory of creativity. In P. E. Vernon (Ed.), *Creativity* (pp. 137–151). Baltimore: Penguin.

Secada, W. G., Chavez-Chavez, R., Garcia, E., Muñoz, C., Oakes, J., Santiago-Santiago, I., & Slavin, R. (1998). *No more excuses: The final report of the Hispanic dropout project.* Washington, DC: U.S. Department of Education. Retrieved from http://eric.ed.gov:80/PDFS/ED461447.pdf

Smutny, J. F. (2001). *Stand up for your gifted child.* Minneapolis: Free Spirit Press.

Smutny, J. F. (2002). Teaching young gifted minority students: Teacher-parent partnerships. *Gifted Education Communicator, 33*(1), 37–39.

Smutny, J. F. (2003). *Designing and developing programs for gifted students.* (A Service Publication of the National Association for Gifted Children). Thousand Oaks, CA: Corwin.

Smutny, J. F., & von Fremd, S. E. (2009). *Igniting creativity in gifted learners, K–6: Strategies for every teacher.* Thousand Oaks, CA: Corwin.

Smutny, J. F., Walker, S. Y., & Meckstroth, E. A. (1997). *Teaching young gifted children in the regular classroom: Identifying, nurturing, and challenging ages 4–9.* Minneapolis: Free Spirit.

Smutny, J. F., Walker, S. Y., & Meckstroth, E. A. (2007). *Acceleration for gifted learners.* Thousand Oaks: Corwin.

Snell, L. (2002). *Special education confidential.* Strasburg, VA: National Right to Read Foundation.

Stanish, B. (1988). *Lessons from the hearthstone traveler: An instructional guide to the creative thinking process.* Carthage, IL: Good Apple.

Swanson, J. D. (2006). Breaking through assumptions about low-income, minority gifted students. *Gifted Child Quarterly, 50*(1), 11–25.

Tavernise, S. (2011, August 25). Young Hispanics' college enrollment rose 24% in year, study says. *New York Times.* Retrieved from http://www.nytimes.com/2011/08/26/us/26census.html.

Thomas. W., & Collier, V. (1997). *School effectiveness for language minority students.* Washington, DC: George Washington University Center for the Study of Language and Education.

Tomlinson, C. A. (1999). *The differentiated classroom: Responding to the needs of all learners.* Alexandria, VA: Association for Supervision and Curriculum Development.

Tomlinson, C. A. (2002). Lessons from bright learners about affect. *Gifted Education Communicator, 33*(1), 41.

Torrance, E. P. (1969). Creative positives of disadvantaged children and youth. *Gifted Child Quarterly, 13*(2), 71–81.

Torrance, E. P. (1977). *Discovery and nurturance of giftedness in the culturally different.* Reston, VA: Council for Exceptional Children.

Torrance, E. P. (1979). *The search for satori and creativity.* Buffalo, NY: Creative Education Foundation.

Torrance, E. P. (1983). The importance of falling in love with "something." *Creative Child and Adult Quarterly, 8*(2), 72–78.

Torrance, E. P. (1985). Who is gifted? *Illinois Association for the Gifted Journal,* 2–3.

Torrance, E. P. (1998). Talent among children who are economically disadvantaged or culturally different. In J. F. Smutny (Ed.), *The young gifted child: Potential and promise, an anthology* (pp. 95–118). Cresskill, NJ: Hampton Press.

Torrance, E. P., Goff, K., & Satterfield, N. B. (1998). *Multicultural mentoring of the gifted and talented.* Waco, TX: Prufrock Press.

Tucker, G. R. (1999, August). A global perspective on bilingualism and bilingual education. *Center for Applied Linguistics Online Digest, EDO-FL-99–04.* Retrieved from http://www.cal.org/resources/Digest/digestglobal.html

U.S. Census Bureau. (2009). Data set: 2009 American community survey 1-year estimates. *American community survey.* Washington DC: U.S. Census Bureau. Retrieved from http://factfinder.census.gov/servlet/STTable?_bm=y&-qr_name=ACS_2009_1YR_G00_S1601&-geo_id=01000US&-ds_name=ACS_2009_1YR_G00_&-_lang=en

U.S. Census Bureau. (2010a). *Language spoken at home.* American Community Survey 1-Year Estimates 2010. Washington DC: U.S. Census Bureau. Retrieved from http://factfinder2.census.gov/faces/tableservices/jsf/pages/productview.xhtml?pid=ACS_10_1YR_S1601&prodType=table

U.S. Census Bureau. (2010b). *Overview of race and Hispanic origin: 2010 census brief.* Washington DC: U.S. Census Bureau. Retrieved from http://www.census.gov/prod/cen2010/briefs/c2010br-02.pdf

U.S. Census Bureau. (2010c). *Race and Hispanic or Latino: 2010—United States —places and (for selected states) county subdivisions with 50,000 or more population by state; and for Puerto Rico 2010 census summary file 1.* Washington, DC: U.S. Census Bureau. Retrieved from http://factfinder2.census.gov/

faces/tableservices/jsf/pages/productview.xhtml?pid=DEC_10_SF1_
GCTP3.US10PR&prodType=table

U.S. Commission on Civil Rights. (2007). Minorities in special education. *A briefing before the U.S. Commission on Civil Rights.* Retrieved from http://www.usccr.gov/pubs/MinoritiesinSpecialEducation.pdf

U.S. Department of Education. (1993). *National excellence: A case for developing America's talent.* Washington, DC: U.S. Department of Education. Retrieved from http://www2.ed.gov/pubs/DevTalent/coverpge.html

U.S. Department of Education. (1998, August). *Talent and diversity: The emerging world of limited English proficient students in gifted education.* Washington, DC: Office of Educational Research and Improvement, U.S. Department of Education. Retrieved from http://www.eric.ed.gov:80/PDFS/ED419426.pdf

U.S. Department of Education. (2012). *Building the Legacy: IDEA 2004.* Washington, DC: U.S. Department of Education. Retrieved from http://idea.ed.gov/explore/view/p/%2Croot%2CI%2CA%2C602%2C30%2C

Valdés, G. (2003). *Expanding definitions of giftedness: The case of young interpreters from immigrant communities.* Mahwah, NJ: Erlbaum.

Van Tassel-Baska, J. (1989). The role of the family in the success of disadvantaged gifted learners. *Journal for the Education of the Gifted, 13*(1), 22–36.

Van Tassel-Baska, J. (2009). Teaching and parenting gifted adolescents. In J. A. Willis (Ed.), *Inspiring middle school minds: Gifted, creative, and challenging* (pp. 15–38). Tucson, AZ: Great Potential Press.

Vygotsky, L. S. (1962). *Thought and language* (E. Hanfmann & G. Vakar, Trans.). Cambridge: MIT Press. (Original work published 1934).

Willis, J. A. (2009). *Inspiring middle school minds.* Scottsdale, AZ: Great Potential Press.

Winebrenner, S. (2001). *Teaching gifted kids in the regular classroom: Strategies and techniques every teacher can use to meet the academic needs of the gifted and talented.* Minneapolis: Free Spirit.

Wyner, J., Bridgeland, J., & Diiulio, J. (2009). *Achievement trap: How America is failing millions of high-achieving students from lower-income families.* Lansdowne, VA: Jack Kent Cooke Foundation. Retrieved from http://www.jkcf.org/news-knowledge/research-reports/

Yoon, B. (2008). Uninvited guests: The influence of teachers' roles and pedagogies on the positioning of English language learners in the regular classroom. *American Educational Research Journal, 45*(2), 495–522.

Index

CORWIN

A SAGE Company

The Corwin logo—a raven striding across an open book—represents the union of courage and learning. Corwin is committed to improving education for all learners by publishing books and other professional development resources for those serving the field of PreK–12 education. By providing practical, hands-on materials, Corwin continues to carry out the promise of its motto: **"Helping Educators Do Their Work Better."**